The
Conflict
Resolution
Syndrome

Volunteerism, Violence, and Beyond

The
Conflict
Resolution
Syndrome

Volunteerism,
Violence,
and Beyond

Alexander Abdennur, Ph.D.

University of Ottawa Press

Canadian Cataloguing in Publication Data

Abdennur, Alexander, 1945-
  The conflict resolution syndrome

Bibliography: p.
ISBN 0-7766-0141-5

1. Volunteers—Psychology. 2. Volunteer workers
in social service—Psychology. 3. Conflict
(Psychology) I. Title.

HM136.A23 1987 302'.08836 C87-090121-4

Book design by Gregory Gregory Limited, Ottawa
Typesetting by Nancy Poirier Typesetting Ltd., Ottawa

Printed and bound in Canada

CONTENTS

1 Introduction and Overview   1

2 The Volunteer Personality:
   A Critical Review of Research   25

3 The Study   43

4 The Conflict Resolution Syndrome   69

5 Volunteers, Volunteerism, and Society   85

6 The Tender Trap   115

   Appendix   129

   Bibliography   133

FOREWORD

A concern with conflict and an interest in finding strategies for its resolution at the social, political, and international levels have increasingly dominated public consciousness and penetrated various academic disciplines. The study of conflict has also constituted a major preoccupation for students of psychodynamics and psychotherapy. The overwhelming concern with the resolution of conflict at the political, administrative, and psychological levels has apparently overshadowed the investigation of conflict resolution as a personal adaptation.

In an attempt to investigate conflict resolution at the personal level, this book examines how the selection of, accommodation to, and construing of a certain situation can be a function of the personal adaptation to the conflict inherent in that situation. The theoretical model presented in this book distinguishes three basic qualitative modes in the process of response to and resolution of conflict: confrontation, conflict reconciliation, and conflict avoidance. The analysis focuses on the third mode of conflict resolution, that of conflict avoidance, treating it as a personality variable, as a personality typology, and as a psychosocial adaptation that can have serious social and political implications. This theoretical model is verified by preliminary psychometric research that supports the assumption that modes of conflict resolution are pervasive within the personality and can be treated as personality variables.

In this study, the investigation of conflict resolution as a personal adaptation focuses on the volunteer movement, because volunteers tend to select freely the roles that are harmonious or consistent with their personalities. The hypothesized modes of conflict resolution are tested on samples of correctional and social service volunteers, and the latter group in particular is found to exhibit conflict avoidance orientations and behaviour.

The author's extensive analysis of the psychological, social, and political aspects of volunteerism has been prompted by the remarkable proliferation of this movement during the past two decades. The rapid increase of volunteer programs in social services and many areas of public life, endorsed and supported by government agencies, has been observed all over North America. For example, the period between 1965 and 1975 alone saw an increase of nearly sixty per cent in the number of persons actively engaged in volunteer work. In 1981, 37 million individuals in the United States and 2.8 million in Canada worked as volunteers, with an estimated value of services of 65 billion dollars for the United States and 3.5 billion for Canada (*Consultation '81*, 1981). The following quotation from a speech by President Ronald Reagan attests to the ideological and political support lent to volunteerism:

> I just wish those who are pessimistic about the future of America could see an overview of this surge of creative and humanitarian action. We believe it should be recognized, encouraged, and promoted. And that's why we established the President's Volunteer Action Awards and brought this year's recipients to the White House.
>
> Ronald Reagan (1982)

This book makes three contributions to the theory of conflict resolution: first, it depicts conflict avoidance, conflict reconciliation, and confrontation as personality variables capable of influencing behaviour at the perceptual, psychodynamic, and cognitive levels of functioning; second, it presents conflict avoidance as a personality typology that is useful in predicting individual behaviour; third, it analyzes conflict avoidance as a psychosocial adaptation that tends to involve ideological and political choices and orientations. Chapter 1 contains an overview of the book together with some important definitions. Chapter 2 contains a critical review of the literature on the personality characteristics of volunteers. The research study is presented in Chapter 3, with the theoretical assumptions, instruments, hypotheses, and results of the study. In Chapter 4, a personality typology based on conflict avoidance is presented. Chapter 5 contains social and political analyses of aspects of volunteerism, and Chapter 6 describes the social and political dangers inherent in conflict avoidance strategies.

As Chapters 1-3 are rather technical in nature, the general reader may choose to skim through them once he or she has grasped the basic theoretical conceptualization. Chapters 4, 5, and 6 are progressively easier to read than the first three and the material therein is, perhaps, more appealing to the general reader who is mainly interested in the psychosocial and political implications of the theory.

The value of a social science theory lies in its explanatory power —in identifying new variables and simplifying complex phenomena.

It is hoped that the publication of this book will motivate others to conduct additional research that can refine the present constructs and further consolidate the theory.

Chapter 1

Introduction and Overview

The way individuals deal with conflict varies markedly with personal dispositions and impinging situational options and constraints. An individual's response to conflict is a holistic one that engages the personality at a deeper level than one's response to ordinary economic and professional decisions. This emotionally deeper and psychologically more pervasive response to conflict is understandable when we consider that, phylogenetically, the prototype of all conflicts is the aggressive challenge. It is well established that aggression tends to mobilize hormonal and neurophysiological processes that engage and affect the organism as a whole. The fact that a large variety of psychosomatic symptoms can be caused by a particular intrapsychic conflict may further testify to the pervasive reaction within the individual as a result of conflict.

Although one's response to conflict may be influenced by the situation, it is, nevertheless, possible to discern certain qualities in the response that are individually specific. We can identify an individual's typical mode of response to conflict by studying his or her behaviour over a period of time, or by observing the individual's reaction to conflict at several levels of behaviour or personality functioning. In this book an attempt is made to identify and account for certain specific modes of response to conflict. These modes are also shown to constitute personality variables capable of influencing the individual's personal and social behaviour. The response to conflict, in the present study, is seen to consist of the process of conflict resolution, a process that involves accommodation and adaptation strategies.

The task of exploring a new personality variable demands a brief account of dispositional concepts in the psychological literature that focuses on personality traits, their relationship to the environment, and their relationship to the personality as a whole.

The Personality Viewpoint

Many personality theorists in psychology employ a person-centred perspective which assumes that behaviour is a function of some enduring aspects or qualities of the person and that the consistencies observed in an individual are to be attributed to some underlying disposition, trait, attitude, or characteristic that an individual possesses. Batteries of personality tests have been created to assess the wide variety of traits that persons are assumed to have in order to explain why they behave as they do.

"Traits" are dispositional concepts that refer to tendencies to act or react in certain ways. In terms of their content, there are many possible kinds of traits. For example, there are *motive traits* referring to the kinds of goals to which behaviour is directed, *ability traits* referring to general and specific capacities and skills, *temperamental traits* such as tendencies towards optimism, depression, and energy, and *stylistic traits* involving gestures and styles of behaving not functionally related to the goals of that behaviour (Lazarus & Monat, 1979).

Trait theorists have approached the task of defining trait categories in quite different ways. For example, although Cattell (1950) included motives within the category of traits, Murray (1938) and McClelland (1951) excluded motives from the definition of traits, traits for them involving characteristic means by which goals are attained.

The major exponent of personality trait psychology is Gordon Allport. Allport (1937, 1961) regarded the trait as the natural unit of description of personality; it refers to actual neuropsychic characteristics that determine the individual's behaviour. Allport distinguished between *cardinal traits, central traits*, and *secondary traits* on the basis of their durability. Trait theory suggests that an individual who reveals a certain trait in one situation is likely to behave in the same way in similar situations. Common traits, according to Allport, when scaled for the population at large, often have normal distribution. Traits may be viewed either in the light of the personality that contains them (i.e., idiographically) or in the light of their distribution in the population (i.e., nomothetically).

Traits were regarded by Allport as the specific structures or units for studying personality. Allport (1961) defined personality as "the dynamic organization within the individual of those psychophysical systems that determine his characteristic behaviour and thought" (p. 28). The phrase *dynamic organization* is used to stress the high degree of integration in personality. *Psychophysical* refers to the "inextricable unity" of mind and body. The word *determine* is very important in Allport's definition. He elaborated on the significance of the term:

> Personality *is* something and *does* something. The latent psychophysical systems, when called into action, either motivate or direct specific activity, and thought. All the systems that comprise personality are to be regarded as *determining tendencies*. They exert a directive force upon all the adjustive and expressive acts by which the personality comes to be known. (Allport, 1961, p. 29)

Another major contributor to trait theory, Cattell (1950), directed his efforts towards systematically reducing the list of personality traits to a manageably small number through "factor analysis." He referred to the obvious traits that can be readily observed as *surface traits*. Statistical analysis revealed that surface traits tended to come in clusters. To Cattell, such groupings indicated single underlying traits which he referred to as *source traits*. Cattell isolated sixteen of these more basic factors and developed a questionnaire, the Sixteen Personality Factor Questionnaire (16PF), to measure them. According to Lazarus and Monat (1979), a prototype of a successful application of trait research is the "Locus of Control" dimension and its measures (Rotter, 1966). The Locus of Control dimension has proved to be of considerable value in the attempts to understand and predict certain individual differences in relating to the world.

The Situationist Viewpoint

The situationists are those psychologists who radically subordinate the role of personality traits as determinants of social behaviour. According to them, what people bring to a social situation is not as important as the characteristics of the situation itself (Bowers, 1973). The situationists' philosophical father is B. F. Skinner, who argued that traits are hypothetical constructs that can stand in the way of adequately analyzing human behaviour (Skinner, 1963). Walter Mischel was one of the most outspoken advocates of the situationist position (Mischel, 1968, 1969). He gathered substantial correlational evidence to support his position that behavioural specificity is more common than most people assume it to be. Mischel (1968) noted that the greatest stability has been found for cognitive and intellectual functions, and the least for personality dimensions such as attitudes to authority, moral behaviour, aggression, and rigidity. He also noted that the inconsistency in personality-related behaviours is not a function of poorly constructed measures, but rather is a reflection of nature. In short, Mischel concluded that there is very little evidence that personality-related behaviours are stable; rather, they tend to show considerable specificity across situations and over time.

Mischel's interpretations and methods have drawn many criticisms. Some have argued convincingly that the studies he reviewed do, in fact, indicate behavioural stability (e.g., Block, 1968; Bowers, 1973; Pervin, 1975). Moreover, the "either-or" nature of Mischel's argument overlooks several important possibilities, namely, that stability could vary for individuals, traits, or situations. Some people could show more behavioural stability than others; certain traits in an individual could show more stability than others; or some situations could create more specificity than others (Bem & Allen, 1974).

The Interactionist Viewpoint

The interactionists' basic premise is that social behaviour results from the interaction between the person and the situation he is in. *Both* personality traits and the situational variables determine social behaviour (Endler & Magnusson, 1976). They think that it is inappropriate to pit personality variables against situational variables in the search for causes of behaviour (Endler, 1973; Phares, 1973).

They argue that personality and situational variables together can explain more of individuals' behaviour than either class of variable considered alone. When situational cues are clear, they will determine behaviour; when they are ambiguous, personality traits will be the primary cause of the way the person acts (Phares, 1973). The person and the situation cannot be treated as two separate and independent entities (Bowers, 1973). Just as the situation influences a person's behaviour, the person influences the situation. One's personality, attitudes, values, dispositions, and so on, will affect his or her view of the situation and thus the way he or she acts in it. Bowers pointed out further that the person determines the situation he goes into. People do not randomly select the situations they enter. Instead, they choose situations which tend to have objectively similar characteristics.

The interactionist position is becoming the prevalent point of view among personality theorists and social psychologists (Penner, 1978). According to Penner, a research strategy that combines the multivariate approach with the interactionist point of view tends to demonstrate that personality variables do play an important role in social behaviour.

The Type Approach

The type approach to personality description is an extension of the reasoning used in the trait approach (Lazarus & Monat, 1979):

> Whereas a variety of traits can be assigned to a single person, and we say he or she has this or that pattern of traits, in the "type" approach a broader, more unifying scheme, that of classification or pigeonholing, is adopted. A person is classified as belonging to a type by the pattern of traits displayed. If the person shares a trait pattern with a large group, he or she belongs to a type, thus simplifying description immensely since each shared trait need not be listed separately for each individual. (p. 106)

A vocabulary of types has existed for thousands of years. Hippocrates, in the fifth century B.C., theorized that the body contained four fluids, the predominance of each influencing personality in a certain way. Among the earliest and best-known contemporary typologies is that proposed by Carl Jung (1933) describing introverts and extroverts. The flow of psychic energy in the introvert is towards the inner, subjective world, and energy in the extrovert is channelled towards the outer, objective world. Although these two attitudes are mutually exclusive, they can fluctuate from time to time in the same individual. Jung believed, nevertheless, that people tended to rely on one attitude more than the other, and that individuals could be typed accordingly.

Jung saw pure types as representing extreme cases and argued that within any one type there is a wide range of potential variation. The fact that introverts and extroverts are frequently thought of as falling along a continuum rather than as representing a dichotomy tends to detract from its status as an ideal example of a typology. In modern typological thinking (e.g., Cattell, 1965; Eysenck, 1952) types are distinguished from each other by being qualitatively different rather than being merely different in degree. Thus Freud's typology of oral, anal, and phallic types is more in line with the concept of typology because these three display qualitatively different properties (Lazarus & Monat, 1979).

The now popular Type A and Type B (Friedman and Rosenman, 1974) personality typology is a good representative of the spatial prototype, as distinct from the continuum prototype. The Type A individual is characterized by an excessively competitive drive, a striving for achievement, by aggressiveness, impatience, hostility, and a strong sense of urgency. The Type B individual lacks these qualities and is more relaxed and easy-going. Friedman and Rosenman have found that about fifty per cent of their samples of urban Americans are true Type A personalities, and forty per cent are Type B personalities. The remaining ten per cent show mixed characteristics. Studies have shown that Type A individuals are almost three times more likely to develop heart disease than Type B individuals and, moreover, that Type A's, having had a first attack, are five times more likely to have a second, and twice as likely to have fatal attacks (Friedman & Rosenman, 1974). The relationship between Type A behaviour and heart disease is largely correlational; the exact psychological and physiological mechanisms linking these variables are not yet fully understood. Friedman and Rosenman's work indicates the importance of personality typologies. They have postulated a simple personality typology which may successfully predict those individuals who are highly susceptible to coronary disease.

Four points can be made to clarify the relationship between trait symptoms and typologies. First, typologies are closely interdependent with trait analyses. There are a number of traits which one must possess if he or she is to be assigned to a given type, say, the anal personality, or the A Type. Thus, trait and type analyses represent a common interdependent style of thinking and speaking about personality structure (Lazarus & Monat, 1979). Second, trait analyses and typologies are based on certain theoretical propositions about personality structure and process. Third, typological thinking in personality appears to be congenial with a global view of personality, whereas trait thinking tends to focus on the measurement of personality attributes. The trait approach assumes that all people possess the same traits but in varying degrees. This approach differs from the type approach which claims that there are classes of people who possess certain characteristics and others who do not. Thus, whereas the trait approach assumes a continuity among people in terms of characteristics they possess, the type approach assumes discontinuity (Penner, 1978). Fourth, since the typological approach categorizes individuals in terms of a limited number of traits, it becomes possible to study individuals as representative of a certain type. The individual who fully reveals the identified traits is often referred to as an ideal example or an ideal type.

Conflict Resolution as a Central Personality Variable

The Oxford Dictionary definition of conflict includes the following: to clash, contend, fight, to come into collision, to be incompatible. Conflict, as a process, can be either internal or external to an individual or to a group. It refers to motivation to engage in two or more incompatible or mutually exclusive activities in a given situation. Within the individual it may exist when a person is torn between different decision options, such as entering university versus taking a job. It also occurs between two or more individuals when parties in a social relationship have incompatible preferences for action. It can occur among groups, such as the conflict between labour and management, between organizations, between individuals and organizations, between component parts of a single organization, and between nations. Conflict can occur at the verbal level, such as when a person wants to speak the truth but fears to offend. It can occur at the symbolic level, as when ideas clash to produce cognitive dissonance at the level of the individual, or ideological conflict at the level of political parties and nations. Conflict can also occur at the emotional or intrapsychic level, as in ambivalence or in the conflict between unconscious and conscious drives and wishes.

Social existence involves a great many conflicts. The individual in society is subject to the demands of the many groups to which he or she belongs and to the requirements of the many roles that need to be performed. The conflict of these groups and roles can also result in conflict at the personal and intrapsychic level. The entire process of the socialization of the child has been viewed as a conflict between the individual and society. Freud (1928) has gone so far as to say that civilization itself is a product of the clash between the incompatible demands of biological drives and social conformity.

Besides its immense political implications, the concept of conflict is particularly significant in areas of personal adjustment and mental health. Clinical studies suggest that psychological conflicts are of central importance not only in neuroses, but also in psychosomatic diseases, sexual deviance, and functional psychoses. Furthermore, psychological conflicts and inadequate ways of resolving them appear to contribute to various forms of social pathology, such as marital and vocational failure, delinquency, crime, and addiction. Processes involved in the resolution of conflict can be viewed as highly similar across all levels of social conflict, and these similarities tend to extend to intrapersonal conflicts as well (Deutsch, 1970).

Conflict always involves a level of opposition, contradiction, and tension and, accordingly, exerts psychic demands on the organism experiencing it. The psychic and somatic costs of conflict as experienced in forms of neuroses, psychosomatic illnesses, and maladaptive behaviour are depicted in extensive clinical and experimental research. A state of conflict, which generates disagreeable tension at any of the intrapsychic, interpersonal, and intergroup levels, tends therefore to motivate a *resolution* of that conflict or an accommodation to it that minimizes the tension generated.

In animal ethology, conflict is resolved by the basic strategies of aggressive attack, escape, and displaced compromises which utilize ritualized postures of threat and submission. The identification of units of behaviour in fight and flight, and in settling territorial disputes, has been taken as evidence that aggressive and escape "drives" are independent of each other but interact to determine the final form of a behaviour pattern (Lorenz, 1966). The two dichotomous drives (attack/escape), which are basic to all conflict behaviour in animals, can also characterize human conflict in its manifold and complex levels. An attack response, or a confrontational response, to conflict is a quality of response discernible at any level: physical (e.g., assaultive posture or behaviour), emotional (e.g., hostility, anger), verbal, or intellectual. Similarly, escape or avoidance responses to conflict can be discerned at all levels, forms such as withdrawal, depression, and denial being at the extreme of the avoidance pole. In actual social life, any specific response to conflict can be viewed as taking a certain compromise position on this confrontation/avoidance continuum, since socially adaptive behaviour rarely assumes an extreme position on either pole. But the compromise itself, or the resolution, can be described in terms of a confrontation/avoidance orientation.

The confrontation/avoidance quality of the behaviour exhibited (i.e., the type of conflict resolution or the type of accommodation to conflict) depends on a number of variables: the nature and strength of the original impulses, situational constraints, and prior experience and socialization in similar situations. In this book I shall argue that a general yet deep-seated personality variable that is relatively independent of previous learning is another determinant of the confrontation/avoidance quality of conflict resolution. This personality variable is predicated on the following principle: although all conflict involves the experiencing of psychic tension, individuals vary in their tolerance or endurance of such tension. It is hypothesized that this factor of varying tolerance of conflict-generated tension plays an important role not only in determining the type of resolution an individual adopts but also in the individual's selection of situations and challenges, and in the attitude he or she takes towards his or her own impulses.

The tendency or capacity for confrontation at the psychological level tends to be positively correlated with indicators of mental health (cf. Labaté & Milan, 1985). Among the conflict resolution responses, denial is the least confrontative. The reliance on denial as a conflict resolution strategy has been associated with the development of many personal adjustment problems, including the development of cancer (Simonton, 1978). Passive-aggressive modes (e.g., covert withdrawal, guilt, and anxiety manipulation) tend to prolong conflict. They preclude the development of a comprehensive consciousness of the problem which is necessary for a healthy resolution of the conflict. In psychoanalytic terms, a neurotic symptom is a compromise between the repressed libidinal wish and the inhibiting anxiety. Psychotherapy attempts to bring the repressed wishes into consciousness, thereby improving the patient's ability to confront them and achieve a healthier resolution.

A confrontative attitude need not necessarily culminate in violent aggression, although it involves a strategy of attack. Often the contrary is true: a confrontative approach can reduce the chances of violence because confrontation tends to enhance the level of consciousness of the situation. Consciousness, in turn, promotes a comprehensive unfolding of the factors involved, a process which leads to a more balanced and better adjusted resolution. Robert Park stated that "only where there is conflict is behavior conscious and self-conscious; only here are the conditions for rational conduct." (Park & Burgess, 1924, p. 578). Consciousness can, therefore, be seen as a by-product of conflict, with the confrontative type of conflict most suited for the development of rationality. George Simmel (1908) and Lewis Coser (1956) described in detail the effects of overt social conflict on group integration, one of these effects being the enhancement of group consciousness.

To summarize, conflict appears to pervade a great many activities in social life, at all levels of behaviour: intrapsychic, interpersonal, intergroup, verbal, cognitive, and emotional. Any type of resolution of conflict can be qualified in terms of a relative position on the attack/escape or the more abstract confrontation/avoidance continuum. This dimension can be viewed as continuous or as dichotomous, depending on the theoretical approach utilized. It will be argued that a confrontative orientation has positive individual and social effects, while avoidance has negative effects. In this book, an avoidance orientation towards conflict is depicted, and then analyzed as the cause for certain modes of behaviour that are socially harmful. This view is presented through a discussion of volunteerism.

Conflict Resolution as a Variable in Volunteering

The growth of the volunteer movement in North America in the past three decades has been remarkable. The vast increase of active volunteers and the proliferation of this activity into a large variety of public sectors is bound to have social and political implications that are of interest to social scientists. The interest of this writer in the phenomenon of volunteering was also stimulated by considerable experience with volunteers in a number of settings, but primarily in the field of criminal justice and corrections: jails, penitentiaries, juvenile and adult probation. In attempting an in-depth and comprehensive understanding of this phenomenon, the conflict resolution dimension suggested itself as a possible explanatory variable in the motivation towards, and maintenance of, a volunteer role. Subsequent speculation further suggested that those volunteers who freely select the types of roles they engage in constitute an ideal ground for the verification of the conflict resolution variable.

Official bodies and agencies have recently opened their doors to volunteers. Why have ordinary citizens responded by volunteering? General social factors no doubt play a role: the shorter work week, free time, worker alienation in traditional full-time employment, the chances for an "apprenticeship," and so on. Such factors may be casually involved in the decision to volunteer, often as contributory causes or necessary conditions. However, sociological factors, by themselves, do not constitute an adequate explanation for volunteering. They fail to account for the impact of opposing social factors which also exist, factors such as the abundantly expanding avenues for the expenditure of free time provided by contemporary society. Moreover, they fail to explain why, within the same social and professional groups, some individuals volunteer and some do not. They also fail to account for the popularity of volunteering in spite of opposing ideological trends, for example, the feminist view that taking on unpaid work represents succumbing to exploitation in a society that measures the individual's worth in monetary terms.

A purely psychological approach, on the other hand, is also inadequate for the explanation of volunteering because personality traits do not express themselves independently of the social context of the individual. Personality factors undoubtedly play a part in civic activity, but they vary from one volunteer to the other and may be as much the product as the producer of the behaviour to which they relate (Bronfenbrenner, 1960).

Failure to attend to situational variables may account for the fact that research has been unable to identify a set of personality factors that characterize volunteers and differentiate them from non-volunteers. As will be demonstrated in Chapter 2, the substantial body of research on the "volunteer personality" is replete with contradictory results. For example, Reddy and Smith (1973) found that six personality traits are common: extroversion, social adjustment, personal autonomy, achievement motivation, flexibility, and conscientiousness. However, other studies indicated traits of a less flattering nature. Smith and Nelson (1975), for example, found that volunteers were likely to be lower than average in terms of their shrewdness and their self-sufficiency.

In attempting to understand the phenomenon of volunteering, we need an approach that attempts to link social factors to personality variables. The question of why certain individuals volunteer can be answered at the psychosocial level, at the level of interaction of personality and social variables. The research described in this book attempts to shed some light on this interplay by examining the interaction of a certain personality variable with the structural demands of the volunteer role. Thus the research seeks to examine the motivation of volunteers initially from the perspective of person-environment interactionism (Bowers, 1973; Endler & Magnusson, 1976, 1977).

From an interactionist perspective, an adequate approach to the understanding of the volunteer's motivation must necessarily involve two inquiries: to find out what there is about volunteers that attracts them to volunteer in particular situations, and to depict the characteristics of specific volunteering situations that have a particular attraction for particular kinds of people. While both of the above aspects are taken into consideration, this book seeks to explore the former personality aspect in greater depth, since it is believed that therein lies the interest and contribution of the research that will be presented. The focus on the individual's choice and selection of the volunteer situation orients research towards the exploration of a personality motivational trait without ignoring the role of the situation or totally departing from an interactionist model. The personality variable that is suggested as the major motivational variable in volunteering is that of conflict resolution, with its extremes of confrontation and avoidance. This variable is seen as more relevant than traits suggested by trait theorists such as Cattell. Also, the conflict resolution variable is seen as pervasive within personality and tends, as will be shown, to generate, influence, and cluster several traits.

The Volunteer in Criminal Justice and in Social Services

The research on volunteers presented in this book was not conceived in a vacuum; no research is. It was directed by my curiosity about why so many individuals were attracted to work without pay with delinquents and criminals. What satisfaction did such individuals obtain by giving of their time and their energy to those who had behaved in an anti-social manner and who often were belligerent, hostile, and resentful, and frequently egocentric, manipulative, and ungrateful? Why did these individuals volunteer to befriend such people, to subject themselves to hostility and opposition? Why would they actively seek a role in the criminal justice system, in settings that are characterized by rigid structures, authoritative and controlling interpersonal relationships, and deprivation of individual freedoms? Why would they attempt to relate warmly to people who had demonstrated contempt for others? By the same token, one might be curious about the motives of those individuals who are prepared to spend a good deal of their time and energy in caring for victims of heredity, disease, and the social system such as the retarded, handicapped, and mentally ill.

Explanations that attempt to account for the motivation of the above-mentioned types of volunteering are limited both in quality and quantity—an intriguing problem in itself (see Chapter 2). Sometimes general sociological factors such as leisure, alienation, or opportunities created by the system for its own functional needs are advanced. Occasionally, psychoanalytic explanations are hinted at, such as the atonement for unconscious guilt or warding off the fear of an affliction by confronting its victims.

However, trait-oriented research appears to have dominated the investigation of personality characteristics of volunteers. A great many of the traits and attitudes that were found to characterize volunteers tend to be too general to explain the motivation for a particular behaviour in a particular setting. Searching for more such traits and characteristics will hardly enhance a dynamic explanation of the behaviour in question. Furthermore, when deeper analysis is sought, traits such as compassion, sociability, sympathy, and tolerance tend to suffer from circularity, as in the case of explaining an individual's aggressive behaviour in terms of his aggressivity. Thus, a great deal of research can serve to "explain away" rather than actually explain certain phenomena.

In this study, the volunteers' response to conflict was examined in an attempt to explore their motivational characteristics and to understand the deep-seated dynamics of accommodation to conflict. It was found that the volunteers' typical mode of conflict resolution could account for certain characteristics found to be common among volunteers. It will be argued that as a personal-environment typology, this conflict resolution variable may have considerable value for our understanding of a wide range of human activities, particularly those related to political affiliation and modes of interpersonal and social conflict. Moreover, the research, by identifying a cluster of volunteer characteristics, raises profound implications for the effects of the volunteer movement on North American social and political life.

For the purposes of the study, voluntary action refers to those kinds of human activity, whether individual or collective, that are performed primarily for reasons other than (a) expectation of direct remuneration, (b) the coercion of law, physical force, economic threats, or other political force, or (c) the compulsion of physiological needs (Smith, 1974). There are several types of voluntary action, each type differing from the others with respect to the kinds of organizations or groups involved, the kinds of activities performed, and the types of individuals who participate. Some of the types involve participants who are not normally labelled as "volunteers" although they act in a voluntary manner. The following distinctions will help clarify and define the type of volunteers that are the subject of the study.

1. *Correctional or Criminal Justice Volunteers*: In this study the terms "correctional volunteers" or "criminal justice volunteers" refer to individuals who are helping or doing things for offenders in the criminal justice system and who are directly involved with their offender clients either in detention centres, prisons, and penitentiaries, or in community criminal justice agencies: adult and juvenile probation, parole, and half-way houses. Self-help offender groups are excluded from this definition of volunteers because an expectancy of direct remuneration or reward is involved in their case.

2. *Social Service Volunteers*: In this study the term "social service volunteers" refers to individuals who are helping others or who are doing things for others, and who directly interact with their clients

in the helping activity. They include volunteers working in hospitals, with the Red Cross, with the physically and mentally handicapped, with the mentally and emotionally ill, and in geriatric homes. This is the most traditional type of volunteer and the one that usually comes to mind when voluntary action is mentioned.

Correctional volunteers have often been placed in the category of social service volunteers (e.g., Smith, 1974). However, a deeper analysis of their role (see Chapter 3) reveals substantial differences from volunteers in purely helping roles.

In addition to social service volunteerism, Smith (1974) suggested other types of voluntary action which when outlined can present an adequate classification of voluntary activities:

3. *Cause-Oriented Volunteerism*: that form of voluntary action which is primarily directed at some kind of public issue, usually at making some kind of specific change in society or the biophysical environment (e.g., consumerism, environmental protection, planned parenthood, minority group rights). The changes focused on are usually humanitarian. The goals of the activity are usually specific and do not involve a major or radical reorganization of the social order.

In some cases the voluntary action involves the use of educational campaigns, peaceful demonstrations, and the information media. The more active forms of cause-oriented movements are directed towards bringing changes to the social structure on such issues as women's rights, unemployment, racism, etc. These qualify more as political movements with different motivation than merely voluntary action.

4. *Consummatory or Self-Expression Volunteerism*: that form of voluntary action which is primarily aimed at the enjoyment of activities for their own sake and for the sake of personal self-expression and self-realization, without any major focus on altruism or political or social change (e.g., country clubs, little theatre groups, social clubs, bowling leagues, etc.).

5. *Occupational/Economic Self-Interest Volunteerism*: that form of voluntary action which is primarily aimed at furthering the occupational and/or economic interests of its participants (e.g., trade unions, professional associations, businessmen's groups, etc.).

6. *Philanthropic/Funding Volunteerism*: that form of voluntary action that is primarily aimed at raising funds and/or distributing them to non-profit and voluntary organizations of all kinds in order to further philanthropic causes in such areas as health, welfare, education, religion, politics, etc. This type of volunteering does not involve direct or intimate interaction with the clients who are the object of concern.

The research will deal only with correctional and social service volunteers. Cause-oriented volunteers will be discussed later on in the book in the context of the impact of volunteerism on North American society. Types 3-6 described above appear to be somehow different from, or lack a certain psychological quality which is found in, social service volunteers. Their approaches tend to be either impersonal, self-serving, or group-serving in contrast to the individual-centred altruism that seems to characterize most social service volunteers. Therefore, the conclusions of the study are limited to the correctional, social service, and partially to cause-oriented volunteers and cannot be generalized to other types of volunteers active on the social scene or to those who volunteer as subjects for experimental research.

In the case of social service volunteerism, it is important to distinguish between traditional volunteerism and new volunteerism. *Traditional Volunteerism* refers to volunteer groups that were prevalent during the last two hundred years in North America, England, and parts of Europe. These groups were usually church-centred and oriented to their own community. They involved middle- and upper-class individuals (predominantly women) who espoused the Christian values of charity and "doing good." The extreme type of traditional volunteerism is the missionary. This traditional type of volunteerism still survives in some social settings; however, it began to decline towards the middle of this century when governments started to expand and formalize social services and to staff them with professionals. *New Volunteerism* refers to the upsurge of volunteerism during the past two decades within most social service agencies. New volunteerism is endorsed and encouraged by governmental bureaucracy and provides a significant proportion of the manpower for many social agencies. Chapter 2 presents a critical review of recent research carried out on various volunteer groups and centring on the personality characteristics of new volunteers.

The Criminal Justice Volunteer in Conflict

The unusual perception of the characteristics of criminal justice volunteers that stimulated this research is described in detail in Chapter 3. In brief, the author's observations of volunteers working in a variety of criminal justice settings led to the suspicion that the primary demand of the volunteer role in corrections may be the reconciliation of conflict. It seemed that the correctional volunteer occupies a social role which aims at the reconciliation of conflict between two opposed social entities: the offender population and the criminal justice system representing the demands of society. The police, the courts, the prison, and the parole system are in direct conflict with the offender. They seek to control or change his behaviour; he seeks to manoeuvre, manipulate, avoid, or obstruct their efforts. The correctional volunteer assumes the role of mediator who must somehow accommodate and reconcile these opposing positions. In observing correctional volunteers, it became apparent that such a role requires an individual who, to a certain extent, is attracted to a conflict situation and who is psychologically able to accommodate opposing views and tolerate conflict. Talking with individuals who came to offer their services as volunteers, the author became aware that many of them evidenced such characteristics. Moreover, those who continued to work as volunteers, in contrast to those whose involvement was short-lived, seemed to be able to accommodate quite readily, even eagerly, to their role as mediators and to be quite at ease in their position between the conflicting parties. Many seemed to relish their roles as conciliators.

The question arose whether the role sought by correctional volunteers might fit their personalities. As suggested by the unity of style postulate (Jaensch, 1938; Frenkel-Brunswik, 1951) and the situation selection implied in the interactionist model (Endler & Magnusson, 1976), the conciliatory role that they selected complemented their personality characteristics. Perhaps, as individuals, they were people who readily identified and empathized with opposing points of view and tolerated and accommodated ambivalence. Perhaps these personality characteristics led them to be attracted to that role. Accordingly, a research project was designed to determine whether the personality characteristics of correctional volunteers are consistent with the conflict reconciliation activities demanded of the individual who works as a volunteer in corrections. If this were found to be the case, it would indicate that their personality traits were psychologically consistent with the structural demands of the role, and it could be argued that traits oriented towards conflict reconciliation (a position between confrontation and avoidance of conflict) might constitute a motivational factor in both the choosing and the maintaining of a volunteer role in corrections.

A typical controversy is bound to arise in this context, namely, whether the traits exhibited are learned through adaptation to the role requirements, or whether they are brought into the role by the volunteer himself. On the one hand, it must be accepted that some learning of skills and changes in some attitudes are bound to take place as a result of taking on a volunteer role in criminal justice. On the other hand, personality traits cannot be completely dismissed, either as motivators for selecting the role or as adaptive enhancers that maintain its continuity. In order to resolve this personality-environment controversy and to assess personality factors independently of the role, an attempt was made to assess conflict-related traits at different levels of personality functioning. Traits such as preference for articulated geometric form at the perceptual level, or the degree of abstraction/concreteness at the cognitive level can hardly be expected to be altered to any significant degree by the volunteering activity. Moreover, the measures used to assess attitudes and preferences are not directly related to the volunteer context. Thus, the accounting for a certain general personality variable that is demanded by the volunteer role, but not generated by it, would tend to confirm that this personality variable is motivationally involved in the choice as well as the maintenance of the volunteer role. Furthermore, by assessing the manifestation of a certain trait at different levels of personality functioning, it is possible to verify the unity of style postulate.

The research focused on an examination of the response of correctional volunteers to measures of conflict at four levels of personality functioning. It was hypothesized that correctional volunteers, in contrast with non-volunteers, would evidence a number of characteristics that would indicate a tendency towards a reconciliation type of conflict resolution: (1) at the emotional level, they would have a high degree of tolerance for ambivalence and an ability to accept two opposed entities; (2) at the perceptual level, they would evidence a preference for less ordered, less articulated, and more open structures; (3) at the cognitive level, they would exhibit a lower level of abstract reasoning or abstract construing of social problems and issues; and (4) at the sociopolitical level, they would tend to reject confrontation or violence as an appropriate solution to problems. The conflict resolution measures are presented in Chapter 3.

The research results tended to support the hypotheses and the assumption that individuals who are attracted to work in the conciliatory role that is required of correctional volunteers are likely to be those who have an unusual affinity for compromise and reconciliation.

Conflict Reconciliation Versus Conflict Avoidance

It was argued that the correctional volunteer tends to serve the demands of the system and the needs of the offender at the same time and functions to reconcile the ensuing conflict between them. Other volunteers who work in the social service field with retarded, handicapped, geriatric, or mental health populations are not involved in the kinds of conflict situations that are experienced by the correctional volunteer. The clients of the correctional volunteer are generally in conflict with the agency that assumes responsibility for them. In contrast, the clients of the other social service fields are typically highly dependent on the agency. Therefore, whereas the correctional volunteer seeks and carries out reconciliation activities, the social service volunteer actively avoids such activities and selects volunteer roles in which conflict is minimal. In effect, it was reasoned that the correctional volunteer's activity can be viewed as *conflict reconciliation* while that of the social service volunteer can be seen as *conflict avoidance.* This hypothesis was supported by the research described in Chapter 3 which found that social service volunteers showed, on conflict resolution measures, a greater tendency towards the avoidance of conflict than correctional volunteers. Non-volunteers scored lowest on conflict resolution measures indicating that they have a relatively higher tendency for confronting conflict.

The Conflict Resolution Syndrome

Predictions about the personality characteristics of social service volunteers were made on the basis of their presumed conflict avoidance orientation—a mode of resolution of or accommodation to conflict. On the assumption that a level of conflict is involved in any social activity, a questionnaire was designed to assess the preferences and attitudes of social service volunteers in relation to various forms of activities. Preferences as to the type of music, films, acting, leisure reading, extrasensory phenomena, religious faith, and metaphysical preoccupations were analyzed in terms of their conflict potential. The preferences of the social service volunteers were predicted to be a function of conflict avoidance choices.

Analysis of the results revealed that, in comparison with nonvolunteers, the social service volunteers consistently preferred low-conflict types of interests. This finding suggests that an individual's tolerance of conflict and his or her mode of adaptation to it is generalizable to many levels of his or her personality functioning. Being a pervasive variable, it is both dynamic and deep-seated, an organizational variable that may be a central motivational force in volunteering as in many of the individual's choices and adaptations. Thus, the preferences of social service volunteers tended to cluster around conflict avoidance. On the basis of the above-mentioned questionnaire and the previous conflict resolution measures, a cluster of seven personality traits that have conflict avoidance as their common denominator was established. This cluster of traits, which was found to characterize social service volunteers and which is seen as a function of a conflict avoidance type of resolution, can also be expected to characterize other similar individuals within similar social and cultural settings. Since conflict avoidance is seen here as a mode of conflict resolution, the seven traits expressing conflict avoidance will be referred to as a *conflict resolution syndrome*. Although the traits involved may constitute forms adaptive to conflict at the individual level, I shall argue that they can be dysfunctional and harmful at the social level. The justification for the use of the term "syndrome" and the description of the cluster of seven traits are presented in Chapter 4.

The Social-Political Impact of Volunteerism

Chapter 5 discusses the sociopolitical impact of social service and cause-oriented volunteers. As we shall see, the impact may be profound. The interaction of the conflict avoidance orientation in volunteerism with social and political factors can have disconcerting implications. The basic tenets of traditional volunteerism are first outlined at the theological, philosophical-social, and practical levels. The major approaches of new volunteerism are also depicted in this chapter, and it is shown that the quality of its social expression is similar to that of traditional volunteerism. It will be argued that, in spite of the adoption of concepts and approaches from social science, concreteness, pragmatism, and anti-intellectualism remain part and parcel of new volunteerism.

New volunteerism is analyzed from the point of view of seven critical perspectives: (1) The thinking and approaches of new volunteerism are seen as one-dimensional in terms of the social theory of Herbert Marcuse (1964). They promote the containing forces of contemporary society rather than bringing about a critical challenge to them. (2) New volunteerism is depicted as a reinforcer of the North American system of pluralism; it helps to crystallize the identities of subgroups, only to reintegrate them within the larger mosaic of competing cultural and minority groups. (3) The movement is analyzed from the point of view of the "neutralization of opposites" process described by Marcuse (Marcuse, Moore & Wolf, 1965). Volunteerism tends to neutralize the beneficial social functions of conflict through moral objectification and "passive" tolerance. (4) The administrative and bureaucratic control of a volunteer is likely to make him an extension of the state. This involves a form of covert domination. (5) New volunteerism in corrections is seen as an additional role in the already overburdened role structure of the criminal justice system. This is likely to activate self-fulfilling prophecies that encourage secondary deviance and dependency. (6) Cause-oriented volunteers appear to be quick to react to social issues with flamboyant and theatrical manners that are essentially non-confrontative. As a result, they tend to take the initiative away from more radical individuals who may be slower to react, but who may be prepared, once they react, to utilize more effective approaches. (7) The intervention of the correctional volunteer can represent, in many cases, a form of psychological parasitism: the volunteer psychologically thrives on the conflict inherent in the offender's situation or personality, but at the same time manages to neutralize and obstruct a healthy dialectical unfolding of that conflict.

In Chapter 6 the mode of aggression often expressed by the conflict avoidant personality is depicted as that of passive-aggression. Passive-aggression is most adaptive to complex formal organizations that provide the tools and the camouflage for this mode of aggression. Also, the conflict avoidant personality by virtue of its recoil from confrontation tends to comply with the contemporary modes of political containment that serve the interests of the power elite. Confrontative approaches that resort to the use of violence are very threatening to those who hold power. The dangerousness of the personality typology in question is further shown to inhere in the inadequate ways these individuals attempt to deal with global issues and problems. They tend to construe global problems in a concrete manner; they tend to seek exhibitionistic, compromised, and superficial solutions; and they appeal to spiritual and moral absolutes rather than to social theory. The inability to confront conflict, according to this analysis, is as potentially dangerous as the ability to attack and wage wars.

The remarkable expansion of social service agencies over the past two decades has been accompanied by an intensive recruitment of volunteers. If such individuals are, as the present study suggests, people who tend to be compromisers, who take a non-confrontative position towards conflict, and who are concrete in their comprehension of social problems, then their ultimate social function may be either to preserve the status quo or to passively give in and adapt to any new social trend. This is achieved through their reinforcing of institutions and political practices that are designed for and oriented towards solving problems by short-term, situational, and piecemeal accommodation based on pragmatism rather than on principle or social design. Such a compromising approach also tends to dissipate initiative for developing innovative or radical solutions to drastic problems that face contemporary society.

Erich Fromm (1941, 1955) has suggested that social institutions and individuals have a reciprocal role in shaping each other. According to Fromm, the institutional arrangements of society tend to produce a personality type or "social character" peculiar to that society. He suggests that the dominant personality type of the society in turn plays a dynamic role in shaping and maintaining the structure and cultural orientation of the institutions it adapts to and controls:

> Social conditions influence ideological phenomena through the medium of character; character, on the other hand, is not the result of passive adaptation to social conditions but of dynamic adaptation on the basis of elements that either are biologically inherent in human nature or have become inherent as a result of historic evolution.
>
> (Fromm, 1941, p. 327)

The institutions of a society have certain personal meaning for their members, and certain social arrangements have particular appeal to certain types of personality. This interaction between institutional arrangements and personality organization can have social implications by virtue of a process of selection and recruitment of personality types who fit and adapt well to certain social institutions and thereby help to reinforce and strengthen the orientation of these institutions. Fromm believed that the authoritarian character found in the lower middle class of pre-war Germany came to prominence in response to drastic economic depression and became, after its institutionalization in the Nazi administration, the social character of the whole country. In this book an argument will be presented that an analogous process may be occurring in volunteerism and similar conflict avoidant movements in North America.

Chapter 2

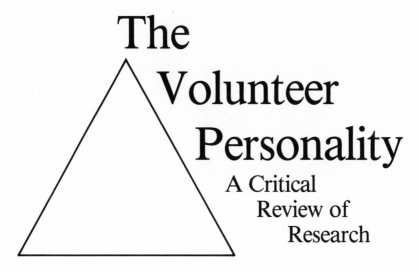

The
Volunteer
Personality
A Critical
Review of
Research

An extensive literature on volunteers has developed during the past two decades. Some studies have demonstrated the value of volunteer activities in terms of economic benefits—the financial savings that accrue from using volunteer rather than paid staff (e.g., Hawrylyshyn, 1978). Other studies have demonstrated the effectiveness of volunteers in modifying the behaviour of clients (e.g., Case & Henderson, 1973; Scioli & Cook, 1976; Andrews & Kiessling, 1980). Still other studies have examined the effects of volunteering activities on the volunteers themselves (e.g., Haan, 1974; Sayre, 1980; Hougland, 1982; Pollock, 1982). Most of the research has focused on three major questions: Who volunteers? Why do they volunteer? How are they affected by their volunteering activity? The literature on each of these questions will be reviewed in this chapter but emphasis will be placed on critically reviewing research on the first question—who are the volunteers? This is the question that has been the focus of most research and which is most relevant to the present study. However, it should be noted that studies of the outcome of volunteer programs frequently conclude that program effectiveness depends a great deal on the characteristics of the volunteers—their attitudes, their interpersonal skills, and the moral values they display (see Andrews et al., 1980).

Experimental Volunteer Subjects

A number of studies have examined the characteristics of individuals who volunteer to act as subjects for psychological research (Rosenthal & Rosnow, 1975). However, these studies have little relevance to the present research. Although the issue appears never to have been studied, it is doubtful whether there is much commonality between undergraduate students "volunteering" as subjects in a research project and individuals volunteering as active participants in a social service endeavour. There is also a growing literature on altruism (e.g., Macaulay & Berkowitz, 1970; Staub, 1978) which has limited relevance to the present study. An examination of that literature reveals little interest in the phenomenon of social service volunteering. However, one study of the literature is relevant to the present discussion. Allen and Rushton (1983) have recently argued, on the basis of their review of the literature on altruism and of their review of the literature on volunteerism, that volunteers compared to non-volunteers have more of the characteristics that have been postulated to underlie the "altruistic personality": empathy, moral standards, feelings of self-efficacy, and emotional stability. ˙

Who Volunteers?

A number of studies have examined the demographic characteristics of volunteers and assessed their personality, attitudes, and values by means of surveys, interviews, attitude scales, and personality tests. Although only a few of these studies examine the characteristics of volunteers in terms of their cognitive functioning, their findings are relevant to the present research and will be reviewed in this section.

1. Demographics

The stereotypical view of the volunteer was that of a middle-aged, middle-class female "do-gooder" or "Lady Bountiful" (Anderson & Moore, 1974). Such a description is no longer valid. Volunteers now represent a broad cross-section of society. No longer are volunteers predominantly middle-aged housewives. On the contrary, approximately sixty-five per cent are students, full-time employees, or retirees (Caldwell, Katz & Levine, 1972). Several studies have found evidence of an increasing involvement of young people under the age of thirty in the volunteer force (e.g., Schnidler-Rainman, 1972; Smith, 1972; Anderson & Moore, 1974). Although the majority of volunteers in some agencies are forty- to sixty-year-old females (e.g., Wallston, 1972), individuals under thirty years of age comprise a significant proportion of the general volunteer population, as high as fifty-one per cent (Caldwell, Katz and Levine, 1972) and seventy per cent (Hillman, 1967). There has also been a major shift in the involvement of males in volunteer work. Although females still predominate, an increasing number of males are involved. For example, a national study of volunteers in Canada (Statistics Canada, 1981) found that men comprised forty-six per cent of volunteers. Nor are the male volunteers primarily from the retired group. Forty-six per cent were less than thirty years old.

Volunteering still appears to be a class-related activity. Approximately sixty to seventy per cent of volunteers are from the middle class (Hillman, 1967; Anderson & Moore, 1974; Durning, 1974). Most are from urban centres, hold white-collar jobs, and have a level of education somewhat higher than average. Married individuals appear more likely to volunteer than do single, widowed, or divorced individuals (Payne et al., 1972; Consultation '81, 1981).

It is interesting to note that conflict between volunteers and staff workers cannot simply be explained away by arguing that they have different backgrounds. On the contrary, there is some evidence that volunteers and staff workers may be very similar in terms of age, marital status, religion, and socioeconomic status (e.g., Almanzor, 1961).

2. Personality

A significant number of studies have examined the personality of volunteers. Most of these studies have compared groups of volunteers with control groups of non-volunteers using a wide variety of personality tests, interviews, and questionnaires. Rather than using non-volunteer control groups, some studies have compared the scores of volunteers with the scores of the normative samples used in the development of the personality measures.

There is little consistency among the studies in terms of the types of volunteers who are examined. Each of the many individual studies has examined the personality of volunteers in a particular area of volunteer activity (e.g., mental health, corrections, or peace corps activities). Fewer than five per cent of the studies have examined the same types of volunteers. Accordingly, caution should be exercised (but seldom has been) in generalizing from individual studies to volunteers in general. Very few studies have attempted to compare the characteristics of volunteers in different volunteer activities. Kegerreis (1977) found that psychometric measures did not discriminate among individuals who performed different types of volunteer activity, but his study was limited to volunteers in a mental health setting. Research comparing volunteers in different settings (e.g., mental health vs. correctional vs. geriatric settings) has received very little attention. A study by Kluge (1974) of "hotline" crisis volunteers found three statistically distinct groups of personality clusters: the self-actualizers, the joiners, and the loners.

In general, researchers appear to view volunteers as a homogeneous group who display several personality characteristics that differentiate them from their non-volunteering peers. The possibility that personality factors can differentiate volunteers from non-volunteers has been the assumption of a considerable body of research. The following broad kinds of personality traits have been thought to be displayed more by volunteers than by non-volunteers.

3. Sociability

It would seem reasonable to assume that individuals who volunteer to devote part of their free time to working with others would be found to be more sociable than those who refrain from such activities. This assumption has often been made by researchers who have attempted to describe the personality characteristics of those who participate in volunteer programs (e.g., Reddy & Smith, 1973). However, there is very little evidence to support the assumption of differences in sociability between volunteers and the general population. There is, in fact, some evidence to suggest that volunteers do not necessarily fit the stereotype of the extroverted, sociable individual, but in fact may tend to be more introverted than non-volunteers. For example, although Smith and Nelson (1975) found that volunteers (Big Brothers and rescue squad workers) were extroverted and group-dependent, a study of college student volunteers in a mental hospital found that they were significantly more *introverted* than non-volunteer controls (Knapp & Holzberg, 1964). Howarth (1976) also found no support for the view that volunteers are unusually gregarious when he studied a large number of female volunteers in a variety of organizations.

4. Social Attitudes

Although there is little evidence to suggest that volunteers are highly sociable in the sense of being outgoing, extroverted, or gregarious, there is some evidence (e.g., Engs, 1973) that they view themselves as being well socialized, as having a strong social conscience, and as being sensitive to and supportive of other people. Thus, in his study of volunteers in the mental health field, Koopman (1973) found that they expressed a greater affinity for close personal relationships than did non-volunteers as measured by the FIRO (Fundamental Interpersonal Relations Orientation) test. They also evidenced a greater number of community-centred values. Hersch, Kulik & Scheibe (1969) found that mental health volunteers were strikingly more sensitive to people and human problems than non-volunteers. Knapp and Holzberg's (1964) study revealed that mental health volunteer students, though more introverted, were more compassionate and sympathetic, and identified more readily with others than did non-volunteers. Tapp and Spanier (1973) found that crisis centre volunteers were more benevolent than the normative population as measured by the MMPI. They also found that the volunteers described themselves as having a greater than average capacity for intimacy. Dawson (1973) found that volunteer peer counsellors at an Australian university were "humanistic" as assessed by the Cattell *Personality Factor Questionnaire*. Unfortunately, only a small sample of twenty volunteers was tested. However, Smith and Nelson (1975), using a large sample (571) of Rescue Squad volunteers, found that, on the Cattell *Personality Factor Questionnaire*, they were more "warmhearted" than non-volunteers (N = 699), and that they more actively sought social approval and admiration from other people. Howarth (1976) found that female volunteers (N = 374) were more trusting of people than female non-volunteer students (N = 1267). Interestingly, Beckman (1972) not only found volunteers to be more benevolent than non-volunteers but also found that they became more benevolent as a consequence of their volunteer work.

5. Self-Concept

Conflicting results have been reported among studies of the volunteer's self-concept. Adsett (1976) found Parents Anonymous volunteers had a more positive self-concept than non-volunteer controls, but Horn (1973) found no such difference in self-image between volunteer and non-volunteer college students. Allen and Rushton (1983) reported that community mental health volunteers perceived themselves as having more self-efficacy than non-volunteers. Andrews et al. (1977) have found that the self-esteem of correctional volunteers is higher than at least one other group of individuals: the offenders they supervise.

6. Autonomy–Independence

A number of studies have found that volunteers view themselves as independent and autonomous. Thus Adsett (1976) found volunteers to a Parents Anonymous group (child-abusing parents) to be more internal on internal-external locus of control scales. An earlier study also found mental health volunteers were more internal than non-volunteers (Beckman, 1972). Tapp and Spanier (1973) also reported that volunteer crisis workers viewed themselves as more independent than their peers. However, Hersch et al. (1969) using the Internal-External Locus of Control scale used by Adsett (1976) and by Beckman (1972) found *no* difference in internal-external scores between mental health volunteers and non-volunteers.

7. Interpersonal Sensitivity and Tolerance

Several studies have noted that volunteers in various agencies appear to be sensitive to people (Chinsky, 1969; Hersch, Kulik & Scheibe, 1969), nurturant (Chinsky, 1969; Chartoff, 1976), benign (Fisher, 1971), sympathetic, and empathic (Tapp & Spanier, 1973; Allen & Rushton, 1983). They also appear to be sentimental (Smith & Nelson, 1975).

Volunteers have been found to be more tolerant and open-minded in their judgement of others (Hersch, Kulik & Scheibe, 1969; Horn, 1973; Engs, 1973; Hobfoll, 1980). They also may be more flexible in their thinking about other people (Hersch, Kulik & Scheibe, 1969; Horn, 1973; Tapp & Spanier, 1973; Engs, 1973), suggesting that they are more adaptable and ready to change (Reddy & Smith, 1973). Some recent research indicates that volunteers may become more tolerant as a result of their volunteer activity (Sayre, 1980).

8. Values

A few studies have attempted to assess the value system of volunteers but there is a lack of consistency in their findings. Thus, Howarth's study of female volunteers indicates that the most prominent characteristic of their personality is their superego. He surmises that the volunteer is "impelled by conscience." Allen and Rushton (1983) found community mental health volunteers to have higher "moral standards" than non-volunteers. Knapp and Holzberg (1964) also found that college volunteers were "morally concerned." However, it is not possible to determine whether volunteers in these studies had achieved a high level of moral development or were merely accepting community values without questioning them. There is some evidence that volunteers are unusually accepting of established values and experience little personal conflict in terms of moral issues (Horn, 1973; Chartoff, 1976). However, Dawson's (1973) study of a small number (20) of Australian volunteers found that on the Cattell 16 PF test they were more radical in their values than the norms for this test. Many were "severely questioning social, community, and political values" (p. 48). However, these results must be questioned in view of the small number of subjects and in view of the fact that the Australian volunteers were actually being compared with Americans who constituted the norms for the test. In general, the results of these studies do not portray the volunteer as a radical individual intent on challenging or changing established values; on the contrary, the volunteer is portrayed as a rather conservative individual who is tolerant of established values but flexible enough to appreciate other points of view.

Surprisingly, few studies have attempted to ascertain whether correctional volunteers differ from their clients in moral development or values. It appears that it is automatically assumed that such differences exist and that they need not be demonstrated. An exception is the series of studies by Andrews and his associates that have found that correctional volunteers differ from their offender clients on a number of value-related dimensions (e.g., Andrews, Wormith, Kennedy & Daigle-Zinn, 1977). Thus, correctional volunteers evidence less identification with criminal others, less tolerance for law violations, more positive attitudes towards the law and the judicial process, and are more accepting of other people. Volunteers in a variety of social agencies appear to have adopted established social values and display socially accepted attitudes and behaviour such as achievement motivation (Hersch et al., 1969; Tapp & Spanier, 1973; Smith & Nelson, 1975), socially responsible behaviour (Horn, 1973; Engs, 1973), maturity (Hersch et al., 1969), emotional stability (Horn, 1973; Allen & Rushton, 1983), and self-control (Engs, 1973). They also seem to be well-behaved (Hersch et al., 1969). Moreover, they seldom evidence a dogmatic or rigidly authoritarian point of view (Horn, 1973; Tapp & Spanier, 1973; Harris, 1969; Sayre, 1980).

As Smith and Nelson (1975) conclude, volunteers seem to be "unsophisticated" and "conservative, respecting of established ideas, and . . . disinterested in rigorous analytical thought" (p. 309). Moreover, they do not seem to be strongly committed to any ideology but tend to be a middle group politically who are best described as "conventional" (Handler, 1968; Haan, 1974).

Discussion

There appears to be little consistency in the results of studies of volunteer characteristics save those pertaining to the previously mentioned area of interpersonal sensitivity and tolerance. Directly contradictory results rather than inter-study agreement are common. Moreover, several studies with various volunteer agencies have failed to find *any* differences between volunteers and comparison groups of non-volunteers (Donahue, 1969; Wallston, 1972; Habenicht, 1977). The conflicting results may be attributable to at least some of the following factors:

1.   The characteristics of volunteers in a wide variety of agencies have been examined. It may not be possible to generalize across those agencies. Different agencies may very well attract different kinds of volunteers.

2.   Researchers have not only studied widely varying kinds of volunteers; they have also employed widely varying measures of personality. The different tests may simply not be measuring the same characteristic. Differences in results across studies may reflect not differences among volunteers but only differences in the measures.

3.   Some differences among studies may be attributable to differences in the non-volunteer comparison groups that were provided. Some studies simply used for comparison purposes the normative population of the test instrument. One cannot determine whether these normative groups include individuals who are themselves volunteers. Moreover, different tests use different normative populations. Accordingly, making generalization across studies employing different measures is highly problematic.

4.   A crucial factor which was mentioned in very few of the studies was selection bias. Many agencies are highly selective in the kinds of individuals they seek and accept as volunteers. Thus, those characteristics which seem to be common to volunteers may reflect not the characteristics of individuals who wish to volunteer, but only the characteristics of those the agency selects. Moreover, different agencies may have different selection criteria. Thus, differences across studies may reflect not differences among volunteers but only differences across the agencies studied.

5.   Personality measures are strongly affected by what the subjects think the researcher wishes to find or what they think they are supposed to or are expected to be like. If volunteers are, as some studies suggest, unusually sensitive to people's feelings and accepting of established views of proper behaviour, they may be unusually sensitive to the demand characteristics of personality research. Interestingly, most of the studies used personality measures in the form of self-reporting inventories which are particularly sensitive to demand characteristics. The subject can readily determine what his answers are likely to say about him and he can readily adapt his responding to what he considers will create the "proper impression." Differences that are found between volunteers may not reflect real differences in personality but, as Hersch et al. (1969) point out, may only reflect what the volunteers think they *should* be like. It should be noted that the volunteer who is working with child-abusing mothers may have a different view of how she should *appear* than would a volunteer working with geriatric patients. Accordingly, the use of subjects from different agencies may simply mask the real characteristics that volunteers share. At least this possibility suggests that researchers should employ somewhat less obtrusive measures.

6.   The possibility that different agencies may attract different kinds of volunteers and thus prohibit generalization across volunteer groups is supported by research which demonstrates that the duration of volunteer participation is influenced more by situational variables than by personal variables (e.g., Turner, 1972; Pierucci & Noel, 1980). These studies indicate that situational variables such as in-service training, supervision, feedback, staff support and the like, rather than personality, determine the likelihood that a volunteer will persist. Differences among agencies on such variables are considerable and they complicate the comparison of the results using different agencies.

In conclusion, the research reviewed does not warrant generalizations about the common characteristics of volunteers which may differentiate them from non-volunteers. In only some areas does there appear to be a reasonable consistency across studies: volunteers appear to be well-socialized, conventional individuals who readily accept established community values and behave responsibly in accordance with these values. They view themselves as sensitive and sympathetic to other people. They are flexible and tolerant of other people's views; they are not strongly committed to any ideology; and they tend not to engage in critical analytical thinking.

The present study attempts to go beyond the assessment of personality traits such as sociability, flexibility, emotional stability, and the like. It also examines variables at the perceptual and cognitive levels such as the need for order or structure and the tendency towards abstract versus concrete reasoning.

It should be noted, however, that the hypotheses of the present study are in accord with the results of those previous studies that have suggested that there are some consistent characteristics of volunteers: conventional, flexible, tolerant, not committed to any ideology, and unlikely to engage in critical thinking. These characteristics are consistent with the assumption of the present study that the volunteer is an individual who is unusually tolerant of ambiguity (flexible), non-radical and non-confrontative in his values and behaviour.

The suggestion that individuals differ fundamentally in their characteristic attitude and response to conflict is supported by research with college students which indicates that an individual's preferred mode of responding to conflict depends not only on the nature and circumstances of the conflict, but also on their personality characteristics. Thus, Bell and Blakeney (1977) found an association between four personality variables (affiliation, dominance, achievement-motivation, and aggression) and modes of conflict resolution (smoothing, forcing, and confronting). More recently in a study of MBA students, Jones and Melcher (1982) found correlations between these modes and other personality variables (affiliation, deference, succorance, nurturance, dogmatism, and Machiavellianism).

In support of the results of the present research, Jones and Melcher (1982) found that students who prefer to smooth over conflict, or attempt to keep conflict from emerging, tend to be affiliative, succurant, nurturant, and are likely to be bound by conventional morality. It would be interesting to determine whether volunteers would be similar to Jones and Melcher's "smoothers" in their response to the psychological tests employed in their study (Edward's Personal Preference Schedule, Rokeach's Dogmatism Scale, and the Mach III Machiavellianism Schedule). It also needs to be determined whether the measures of modes of conflict resolution used in the above three studies (response to proverbs) correlate with the measures used in the present study to indicate the individual's characteristic attitude and response to conflict. Regardless of the degree of similarity, the studies support the view that individuals differ in their preference for particular modes of response to conflict.

Motivation

The literature on volunteers contains many reports about why individuals devote their leisure time to unpaid activities through which they provide service to others. Most of these reports are simply speculative or commonsensical or trite generalizations about the presumed motivation of volunteers. However, several reports are based on research that has attempted to obtain empirical information on the volunteers' motives for volunteering. In most instances this has entailed simply asking samples of volunteers to self-report their motives and goals or has entailed asking them to rank order a number of possible motives on how they apply to them.

Several major categories of possible motives have been identified by various studies, and the emphasis on certain motives tends to reflect the particular interests of various researchers. Although researchers have tended to describe the categories as independent, they are clearly overlapping. The reason for these overlapping categories is the use of different terms by different investigators to refer to basically similar motives.

Some volunteers appear to be motivated to become involved in voluntary activity only as a means of occupying their spare time (e.g., Guyatt, 1974). Volunteering may simply be a leisure-time activity. Some may be engaged in volunteer activity because it provides them with valuable work experience or with opportunities to establish a relationship with an organization that may later provide employment. Thus, volunteering may not be entirely nonprofessional, but may be more realistically viewed as "preprofessional" (Barr, 1971; Guyatt, 1974). Volunteering, therefore, may not be purely altruistic but may be motivated by the opportunity it presents for personal gains. Researchers have identified a number of personal gains that can motivate volunteer service, including social approval (e.g., Feinberg & Sundblad, 1971; Knowles, 1972; Heckman, 1974). Some volunteers may be motivated by various internal rewards including enhancement of one's self-esteem (Knowles, 1972; Guyatt, 1974; Steiner, 1975; Gandy, 1977). Others may volunteer to escape alienation and obtain companionship (Heckman, 1974; Guyatt, 1974). The opportunity for personal growth that social service can provide may also motivate many volunteers (e.g., Heckman, 1974). One may well wonder whether volunteers see themselves as having just as much to gain from their volunteer service as do the clients who are supposed to gain from the service provided by the volunteers.

The motivation for volunteering may also relate to the individual's wish to help people and to provide service to others (Heckman, 1974; Guyatt, 1974) and may reflect the volunteer's commitment to act in socially responsible ways (Steiner, 1975; Algar, Hug & Lambert, 1975). It may also represent the volunteer's wish to feel that he or she is complying with (or to be seen to be complying with) a "work ethic" (Steiner, 1975).

Interestingly, the view that the volunteer is motivated by strong political or social ideals, or by religious principles (Barr, 1971; Reddy & Smith, 1973), has seldom been supported by research (Handler, 1968; Heckman, 1974; Steiner, 1975). Personal gains rather than social, political, or religious principles appear to engender volunteer activity.

It must be noted that in almost every instance the foregoing studies have simply asked volunteers to report their motives. One cannot determine the degree to which their responses reflect their genuine motives rather than those which they may feel they *should* report, i.e., those that they may feel are socially acceptable or "in vogue." Moreover, the present approach to the question of motivation assumes, rightly or wrongly, that the respondents are not fully aware of the motives that determine their behaviour.

The present study derives from a different conceptualization of the motivation of volunteers. Rather than seeking the volunteers' explanation of "why" they volunteered, an attempt is made to determine whether their volunteer role is consistent with basic personality factors at the perceptual, cognitive, and sociopolitical levels. This study postulates that individuals are motivated to seek situations and roles that are consistent with their basic personality needs and to avoid situations that are not harmonious with those needs. The volunteer's role enables him or her to achieve harmony between his or her personality needs and his or her social activities. In effect, this study postulates that basic personality factors have motivational properties that dispose the individual to seek situations and social roles that are harmonious with these factors.

Effects of Volunteering on Volunteers

Most of the studies on the characteristics of volunteers have been content to measure the personality, attitudes, or values of groups of volunteers taken from the roster of a particular voluntary agency without attempting to differentiate between experienced volunteers and novitiates, or between individuals who express an interest in volunteering and those who actually become volunteers, or between highly active and inactive volunteers, or between volunteers who persist and those who drop out.

It has been noted earlier that volunteers may not be a homogeneous group, that different types of individuals may be attracted to different kinds of volunteering agencies or activities, and that these factors must be considered when attempting to describe the "volunteer personality." It is also necessary to note that there may be differences within a particular agency's "volunteers" depending on when they are measured. Some of the following research provides evidence that a volunteer's involvement and the kind of activity in which he or she is involved, as well as the characteristics of the setting, can influence the volunteer's attitudes and values.

Several studies have yielded evidence that volunteers may personally benefit from their volunteering activity. Thus, Kelly (1974) found that college student volunteers who worked with retarded children evidenced a positive change in their self-concept. Holzberg, Gerwitz, and Ebner (1964) and King, Walder, and Pavey (1970) also found that college students working as volunteers increased in their self-acceptance. Similarly, Sager (1974) found that youths involved in voluntary activity with retarded children also improved in self-esteem, tending to feel more valuable and worthwhile and to be more self-satisfied, self-accepting, and self-confident.

However, the results of research on the effects of volunteering on the volunteers are highly inconsistent and contradictory. For example, whereas Miller (1974a) found that 78 university students became significantly more *internal* (on locus of control measures) after three months of experience in working with hospitalized patients, McKian (1977) found that 52 undergraduate volunteers in the mental health field became more *external*.

Some studies failed to find any differences in volunteers as a consequence of their volunteer activities. Turner (1972) found that attitudes and personality traits of university student "hotline" volunteers changed little as a result of twelve weeks of experience. Starr (1970) found that the eighteen-month cross-cultural experience of Peace Corps volunteers had only superficial effects on them. Recently, Hougland (1982) found that the impact of volunteers' activity on their perception of their ability to influence community affairs was much weaker than is generally assumed. Boyd (1977) found no significant changes in college student volunteers working in one-to-one relationships with young children. Arkell (1975) also failed to find any significant differences in self-esteem or attitudes among school students who participated as tutors for younger students.

The results of the negative finding studies appear to be at odds with a large number of studies that have demonstrated the "helper-therapy principle" (Riessman, 1965), which holds that helping behaviour contributes to changes in the helper (e.g., Cloward, 1967; Hassinger & Via, 1969; Fleming, 1969; Frager & Stern, 1970; Landrun & Martin, 1970; Gartner, Kohler & Riessman, 1971; Ross & McKay, 1976).

Regarding the studies that reported insignificant post-volunteering effects of the role on the volunteer, one might wish to question whether the length of the volunteer's exposure to the role was sufficient to precipitate such effects. Moreover, as Starr (1970) has argued, volunteer activities may be such that no change should be expected to occur because the volunteer's role may be so limited by the agency that volunteers are protected from the situations and experiences that would lead to such changes. Finally, it is likely that volunteer experiences affect volunteers differently. Some may be changed positively as a result of their experience, others negatively, and some not at all. These differential effects summated in group data may cancel each other out, masking any real changes that do occur.

The evidence for change in the volunteer's personality or cognitive style is tenuous. Still equivocal but somewhat more consistent support has been found for the view that volunteers' attitudes and moral values may be modified as a consequence of their volunteering activity. Thus, Holzberg and Gerwitz (1963) found that attitudes about mental illness were modified as a function of volunteer experience. Beckman (1972) found that mental health volunteers changed in several ways as a result of their experience in volunteer activity in a psychiatric hospital. They became more paternalistic and humanistic in their attitudes towards psychiatric patients. They became less authoritarian and less likely to view the psychiatric patients as inferior. Chinsky (1969), and Hobfoll (1980) found that volunteers developed more favourable attitudes to and were generally more positive in their regard for their clients as a consequence of participating in volunteer work.

Haan's (1974) study of Peace Corps volunteers found that they became more politically liberalized, more intraceptive, and more likely to evidence principled moral reasoning following their experience. Holzberg, Gerwitz, and Ebner (1964) demonstrated that students involved in one-to-one helping relationships with psychiatric patients also changed in their moral judgements. They became more tolerant of sex and aggression. King, Walder, and Pavey (1970), using the same moral judgement measure as Holzberg, found that volunteers in a psychiatric setting changed in moral judgement (became more tolerant of sex and aggression), but the difference failed to reach statistical significance.

A study of changes in college student volunteers in a mental hospital setting has important implications for the present discussion. Beckman (1972) found that following their volunteering activity in a mental hospital, volunteers came to adopt the ideology of *both* non-professional hospital staff and mental health professionals. Beckman points out that these views are antithetical and notes that the volunteers are identifying with two directly opposing attitudes "without being aware of the basic paradox between these viewpoints." She concludes that volunteers lack the ability to discriminate between opposing viewpoints (p. 89).

The conflicting results of research on change in volunteers can in some ways be understood in terms of the theoretical assumptions of the present study. It is reasonable to expect that changes in specific attitudes may occur as a result of volunteering. Attitudes towards sex, certain types of crimes, mental illness, and the like can undergo change as a result of close interaction between volunteers and their clients. Changes in self-esteem, self-confidence, self- and other-acceptance might be expected as a consequence of exposure, knowledge, and experience. However, it is less likely that fundamental changes in basic religious or social values would be engendered by volunteering. In the present study pervasive value orientations are assumed to be a function of underlying organizational variables and are thought to be modifiable only slightly by the experience of volunteering. In this context, some personal observations made by the author while examining a student volunteer summer project in Germany are worth noting. Students came from several European countries through a student organization and worked in an institution for the severely mentally retarded. Their attitudes towards the institution were assessed through a questionnaire by one of the counsellors on initial exposure to the institution and two months later. Those students who were initially opposed to the practice of continuing care for such individuals tended to maintain the same attitude after two months of working with them. The practice was still seen as a waste of effort and money. Subjects who initially perceived the institution as a humanitarian operation tended to continue endorsing the humanitarian importance of the institution and some of them indicated that their work with the retarded was psychologically rewarding and spiritually elevating.

Conclusion

Given the inconsistent and often directly contradictory results of the studies reviewed in this chapter, it is difficult to summarize or even make sense out of the research on the characteristics of volunteers. However, some tentative generalizations seem to be suggested by the research results. Volunteers comprise a wide variety of individuals from different walks of life and different sociological strata, but the majority appear to be middle-class females from urban centres who hold white-collar jobs and have a higher than average level of education. Thirty- to forty-year-old married females still appear to predominate, but a major shift has occurred recently in the direction of greater involvement by females and males under thirty years of age.

Volunteers generally appear to be well socialized individuals who view themselves as sensitive to other people, and as sympathetic, compassionate, nurturant, and benevolent. They appear to be rather conservative in their social and political views, and tend to accept with little analytical thought or criticism the conventional and established views of their community. They also appear to be unusually flexible in their attitudes, tending to be tolerant of other people's views. Their attitudes appear to be significantly influenced by the values they are exposed to in their volunteer work. Their ideological positions seem to be neither strong nor clearly thought out.

In general, there appear to be more contradictions than agreements in the results of research on the characteristics of volunteers. This may be due not only to the methodological problems that have been pointed out (sampling problems, demand characteristics, etc.), but also to the fact that researchers have examined relatively superficial characteristics of volunteers and have failed to consider person-situation interaction factors. The present study is concerned with more basic characteristics of volunteers and derives from a particular conceptualization about the interaction between the individual's characteristics and the requirements of the situation in which he or she chooses to volunteer.

Chapter 3

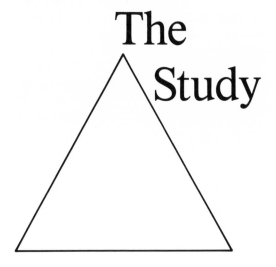
The
Study

The Role of the Criminal Justice Volunteer as Conflict Reconciliation

The use of volunteers in the criminal justice system is at least as old as the concept of corrections itself. It was largely through the philanthropic efforts of such pioneers as John Howard, Elizabeth Fry, and John Augustus that the correction as contrasted with the punishment of criminals became a legitimate, formally recognized process. Ironically, as the various social services became professionalized towards the middle of the century, the role of the private citizen volunteer was virtually eliminated from the correctional system. Sophisticated social service systems required manpower with specialized skills, a certain level of education and training, and carefully screened personnel.

Corrections were no exception. The training and skills of the ordinary citizen came to be seen as inadequate for a system requiring an efficient and effective level of offender control and rehabilitation. Corrections, it was believed, had to be professionalized.

During the 1960s, however, the use of volunteers came full circle. Whereas volunteers had been viewed negatively by criminal justice personnel, they came to be seen once again as important, even essential components of the correctional process. Despite the continuing resistance from some professionals, most jurisdictions, at least in North America, have accepted the re-entry of volunteers into the criminal justice system. The increasing use of volunteers in criminal justice is documented in many surveys. For example, more than 15 per cent of the total probation caseload in the province of Ontario, Canada, is supervised by volunteer probation officers (Ministry of Correctional Services, 1984). It is estimated that in Canada the number of current correctional volunteers working with federal institutions is almost equivalent to the number of incarcerated federal prisoners (Correctional Services of Canada, 1986).

A substantial body of literature has developed describing the programs and services provided by criminal justice volunteers and the methods and criteria for their selection and training. Recently, some systematic evaluation research has been conducted to assess the different forms of deployment and organization of criminal justice volunteers and to evaluate the effectiveness of volunteers as compared with professionals (e.g., Andrews & Kiessling, 1980). This emerging population of unpaid workers, by virtue of their increasing number, the institutionalization of their role, and their official and public endorsement, is expected to exert a substantial impact on criminal justice.

This study attempts to determine whether criminal justice volunteers evidence personality characteristics that are likely to make them more prone than other individuals to seek volunteer work in correctional settings, characteristics that would enable them to readily accept and adapt to the peculiar demands of the correctional setting and to persist in their volunteer role.

The research is not simply an empirical descriptive study aiming at the identification of the personality characteristics of volunteers. On the contrary, the hypotheses that are tested in the study derive from a conceptualization of the structural demands of the correctional setting and are based on the assumption that individuals tend to choose to engage in activities in which the roles they play are psychologically consistent with their personalities.

Specifically, it is assumed that the volunteer in corrections must serve as an intermediary between two opposing forces: offenders and the criminal justice system. The correctional volunteer's role requires that he or she serve as a mediator or a conciliator. It is hypothesized that correctional volunteers are likely to be individuals who are psychologically well suited to their role of conflict reconciliation because they have a high tolerance or an affinity for such activities.

An offender, by virtue of his behaviour, is in conflict with certain social norms, with certain members of society, and with agencies of the criminal justice system responsible for controlling his criminal behaviour. At the behavioural level, what opposes the offender's criminal endeavours in contemporary North American society is seldom the ordinary citizen or the victim. On the contrary, the agencies of criminal justice constitute the actual force with which the offender has to contend. Thus, a substantial portion of the offender's energy—his conscious attitudes of opposition, his psychological attitudes of hostility, defiance and apprehension, his actual efforts at concealment and manoeuvring—is directed against the obstructing agencies of criminal justice. At the forefront of this opposing camp is the police, an agency that has a legal monopoly on the use of physical force as a means of control. The courts, prisons, and parole agencies play various roles in the process of obstruction and containment of the offender. Rehabilitation-oriented agencies of the system such as probation and after-care are also in conflict with the offender. Their support is conditional on the offender's good behaviour, and they hold the ultimate threat of re-incarceration. The offender's reaction to them is usually that of opposition. Therefore, the offender and the agencies of the criminal justice system are in a state of conflict at the organizational level and at the psychological level as well.

Between these two opposing entities, the correctional volunteer carries out activities that are consistent with a conflict reconciliation role. The volunteer deploys personal efforts and resources in order to minimize the conflict between the offender and the agencies of criminal justice. Volunteers frequently intervene to help the offender spend a smooth and trouble-free imprisonment, to make an early parole, to find employment, and to "keep out of trouble" when on his own. Moreover, volunteers often compromise or "humanize" the formal stipulations of the system by interceding with authorities on behalf of the offender and asking for a "break" or "another chance" so that the offender, with the volunteer's help, can prove his worthiness. Volunteers who are given certain controlling authority, as in the case of some probation volunteers, often tend to exercise their authority only after exhausting all the counselling and other supportive means at their disposal. Thus, by their efforts to curtail the offender's criminality through befriending and assisting him, correctional volunteers may shelter the offender from the harshness of formal stipulations and from the authorities who may be enforcing them. At the same time, they help to ease the pressure on the criminal justice system and indirectly enhance its credibility, since their involvement implies a level of endorsement and legitimation of it. Viewed from this perspective, the volunteer tends to play a conflict reconciliation role that mediates between the criminal behaviour of the offender and the authoritative controlling and punishing functions of the criminal justice system.

A similar mediation or conflict reconciliation process appears to be operating at the psychological level. Correctional volunteers must identify and empathize with both parties if they are to maintain their role as volunteers. They have to support the criminal justice agency as an expression of society's values. At the same time, they must empathize with the offender as an individual who is, to a certain extent, a victim of his circumstances and environment. Individuals who totally identify with the punitive or controlling role of criminal justice are unlikely to take on a volunteering role or to find acceptance by the offenders if they do become involved. In contrast, those individuals who identify completely with the offender either as a celebrated victim or as a social rebel seldom maintain their position as volunteers in criminal justice because they are likely to clash with the officials and to be discouraged by a poor response from their offender "clients," whose anti-social behaviour is often tied to egocentric personal gains and not to identification with notions of social justice.

Extremist individuals are, therefore, unlikely to continue in such a role. The volunteer who continues to occupy and conform to the established role is required (and must be able) to identify with both the system and the offender. In rationalizing their role, volunteers may legitimize the criminal justice system to themselves by accepting the fact that its demands are essentially isomorphic with those of society. They may view the offender as a disadvantaged individual who has his basic rights, one of which is to receive fair treatment from the system and to be able to negotiate concessions and structured advantages with it through good behaviour.

Thus, the role of the correctional volunteer as expressed in present-day North America may be seen as requiring a psychological capacity to accommodate and reconcile two contradictory sets of feelings and attitudes in relation to help versus control. The role may require individuals with unusual tolerance for ambivalence and compromise. It is suggested in this study that these psychological qualities are not only dictated by the role as role requirements but are also attributes of the individual who seeks the role and is able to conform to the demands of the correctional setting.

The Role of the Social Service Volunteer as Conflict Avoidance

The correctional volunteer's involvement in the reconciliation of two conflicting camps (the offender and criminal justice) involves a certain level of exposure to conflict and an ability to cope with conflict, but within the context of reconciliation. However, in the case of the social service volunteer, such conflict is not apparent. These volunteers are more likely to be engaged in helping and supportive relationships rather than in reconciling conflict between two opposing camps. They respond to conflict in our society (e.g., affluence-poverty, health-illness, power-impotence, intelligence-retardation) by doing service to the individuals on the losing side of these conflicts (poor, intellectually or physically handicapped, and underprivileged), not by attempting to confront and eliminate the causes of conflict as a more radical,[1] confrontative individual might do. They do not attack the source of the conflict in a confrontative manner. They avoid it or focus on minimizing its effects. Doing so may actually help them to deny the conflict or at least enable them to feel that they have reduced its severity. Their espousal

---

[1]It should be noted that in this book the term "radical" will be used to refer to a relatively high degree of confrontation with the basic causes of a problem regardless of any political connotation. A person can radically confront a physical, an interpersonal, or a social problem, and in doing so he may endorse left wing, right wing or apolitical approaches.

of socially critical views is more likely to serve as a public justification for their volunteering involvement or to generate enthusiasm for serving the needs of their immediate clients or the volunteer agency rather than to be a manifestation of deeply experienced conflicts that motivate confrontative responses.

If the correctional volunteer deals more directly with conflict, he or she does so not in a confrontative way as might a more radical individual, but through avoidance of the conflict by attempting to smooth it over, by compromise and reconciliation. The correctional volunteer attempts to avoid conflict by resolving it, but at least he deals with it. The social service volunteer, in contrast, avoids dealing with the conflict almost entirely. Instead, he or she focuses on its victims. While both are assumed to be conflict avoiders, the social service volunteer is more extreme on the confrontation-avoidance continuum. The correctional volunteer, it is reasoned, can also be placed at the avoidance end of the continuum but not so far as the social service volunteer. His avoidance of conflict is less extreme and is managed by compromise and reconciliation as distinguished from the relatively more confrontative mode of the radical individual and the extreme conflict avoidance response of the social service volunteer.

Non-volunteers are expected to reveal the lowest tendency towards reconciliation and avoidance of conflict. It is reasoned that non-volunteers have not taken the trouble or exerted the effort to engage in a volunteering activity that involves mediation. A choice not to intervene as a volunteer may, among other things, represent an implicit preference for a more radical confrontation with that problem. A level of inaction towards a certain social problem may therefore represent a tacit refusal of limited or superficial intervention and a readiness or capacity for confrontative action. Conversely, the enthusiastic choice and readiness to participate in limited and superficial action may represent an avoidance of a radical confrontation with the problem. Thus, the volunteer's enthusiasm for limited action (the "do something about it" approach) is seen to represent a compensatory front that serves to mask an underlying avoidance attitude towards radical forms of intervention.

In short, it is expected that social service volunteers would evidence the greatest tendency towards the avoidance of conflict. Non-volunteers are expected to evidence the lowest tendency towards the avoidance of conflict (i.e., score highest in the direction of confrontation). Correctional volunteers (reconcilers) are expected to score somewhere in between.

Role Versus Personality

The question as to whether the hypothesized characteristics of the volunteer are attributable to role obligations, that is, to situational factors, or are actually the expression of more enduring and pervasive personality characteristics can present a chicken-egg controversy. A plausible way out of this controversy is to argue that the influence of the volunteer role is relatively minor and neither central nor crucial in the individual's life. The volunteer's work may have minimal or no importance to his or her career or social status, or in terms of the investment of time. Accordingly, the demands and expectations of this secondary role may exert only a minor and situationally specific influence on the volunteer's personality, merely stimulating the deep-seated and enduring personality characteristics pertaining to conflict resolution. This affinity for a certain mode of conflict resolution may constitute the primary motivational component in both the selection and the maintenance of such a role.

As suggested in Chapter 1, an attempt to measure motivational factors independently of the situation would be to determine whether correctional and social service volunteers evidence an affinity for conflict reconciliation and conflict avoidance not only in their volunteer work but in other aspects of their behaviour as well. Thus, one could examine whether a volunteer's mode of conflict resolution is consistent across different levels of his or her personality (perceptual, cognitive, attitudinal, and emotional).

Unity of Style

The generalizability of variables related to conflict resolution from one level of personality to another may be construed from a holistic approach or, more specifically, from the "unity of style" postulate. Jaensch (1938) postulated a unity of style within each individual such that testing his or her performance at one level of functioning (e.g., perceptual) would yield information about his or her functioning at other levels (e.g., cognitive, social). He postulated that the individual functioned in essentially the same way at each level. For example, he found that the ambiguity manifested at the elementary level of sensory perception was also present at the complex cognitive and social levels of an individual.

The issue of the unity of style was later investigated by Frenkel-Brunswik (1949, 1950, 1951), who attempted to develop a perception-centred approach to personality that assumed that generalizations could be made from the field of social perception to personality organization. Frenkel-Brunswik postulated that there are underlying or "formal" personality variables that can account for the consistency of the individual's functioning in various spheres (perceptual, emotional, cognitive, social). These variables, she argued, are more deeply embedded (closer to the physiology) and more generalizable than specific psychodynamic "content" variables such as empathy, guilt, hostility, and the like. Being more pervasive within the personality, they tend to influence the quality of a great many choices, responses, and adaptations.

Frenkel-Brunswik's perspective allows for the study of personality from the relatively "neutral" area of perception. She argued (1950) that this approach has several advantages. It permits greater accessibility to experimental verification than is possible with social and motivational variables. It allows for greater conceptual clarity in revealing the interrelatedness of the social, motivational, perceptual, and possibly the physiological aspects of the personality. For example, a tendency to cling to definite moral views or habits, which psychodynamically may be viewed as a protection against drive impulses, may be related, at the perceptual level, to intolerance of deviation from symmetry. The approach also suggests the establishment of measures that are less likely to be distorted by self-censorship, a distortion that may occur when attempting to assess the individual's functioning in sensitive social areas.

If modes of conflict resolution (confrontation, reconciliation, avoidance) are aspects and expressions of the personality style of an individual, then they should be reflected in the role that is freely chosen and entertained. Thus, finding consistency between an individual's mode of conflict resolution and the requirements of a volunteer role will confirm that the conflict resolution mode is a motivational variable in the choice and maintenance of that role.

The Identification of Conflict Resolution Measures at Different Personality Levels

Before stating the specific hypotheses of the study, it is necessary to define the selected measures of conflict resolution considered at the following major levels: the psychodynamic level, the cognitive level, the perceptual level, and the social-political level.

1. At the Psychodynamic Level

Conflict resolution can be measured by the relative tendency to tolerate ambiguity and ambivalence. Intolerance of ambiguity is indicated by dichotomous and "black or white" choices and attitudes. The *Intolerance of Ambiguity Scale* (Budner, 1962) was used to measure tolerance for ambivalence in its broad manifestations. This scale is designed to measure the degree to which individuals tend to perceive ambiguous situations as threatening or undesirable. An ambiguous situation is one which cannot be adequately structured or categorized because of the lack of sufficient cues. Whereas some individuals view such situations as pleasurable, others experience them as a threat.

The validity of the scale has been supported by research demonstrating its correlation with other tests of intolerance of ambiguity (O'Connor, 1952; Eysenck, 1954; Saunders, 1955). Other validity studies have found satisfactory inter-judge agreement on ratings (Budner, 1962). The reliability of the scale has been found to be satisfactory (.85; Budner, 1962). Finally, a number of studies have found the scale to correlate with measures of other characteristics that are theoretically related to intolerance of ambiguity: conventionality, belief in divine power, religious dogmatism, and favourable attitudes towards censorship (Budner, 1962).

2. At the Perceptual Level

If the external visual form of an object is chosen as the medium of perception, then conflict resolution can be assessed by the relative preference for ordered, articulated structures and forms. Such individual preference expresses a certain compromise between highly ordered forms at one extreme and totally chaotic ones at the other.

For example, some would prefer casually drawn geometric figures to perfectly drawn or articulated ones.

A Form Articulation Test was constructed for the present research in order to examine the possibility that individuals in the various groups differed in their preference for well-defined and structured forms as opposed to poorly defined and unstructured forms. The test required the subjects to indicate their preference for geometric figures that varied markedly with respect to form articulation. The figures were selected from the *Welsh Figure Preference Test* (WFPT; Welsh, 1959). This test was found to discriminate effectively between artists and non-artists and to a lesser extent between conservatively oriented individuals and liberal, self-expressive ones.

Sixty simple geometric figures were chosen and arranged in thirty contrasting pairs. Each pair consisted of two figures which were identical except in the degree of their form articulation (perfection or exactness of form). Thus, a highly articulated figure was contrasted with the same figure with less articulation. Only pairs that could be readily differentiated in form articulation by an independent judge were included.

The subject was asked to indicate which figure he or she preferred in each pair. The choice of closed, perfectly drawn, densely shaded figures was taken as a preference for articulated and structured form (high form articulation). The opposite choice was taken as a preference for imperfectly articulated form (low form articulation).

3. At the Cognitive Level

At the cognitive level, conflict resolution may be assessed through the relative utilization of abstraction in the individual's intellectual confrontation with social problems and issues. Abstraction tends to delineate, differentiate, and categorize attitudes and beliefs. The process of abstraction can simplify and clarify a certain problem or issue, and in this manner abstraction can help in solving problems. However, when an abstract opinion or position is taken, it becomes less amenable to concessions and compromises. In the abstract approach, differences become part of an integrated and unified position bound by universalized values and principles, and this makes compromise difficult. Conversely, a concrete practical approach tends to isolate differences through operationalizing and quantifying them which, in turn, allows for the development of practical measures for solving and reconciling the differences. Coser (1968), writing from a sociological rather than a cognitive perspective, states that:

> Intellectuals who transform conflicts of interest into conflicts of ideas help provide public justification of conflicts and hence to make them more intense. Conflicts may involve the pursuit of personal interests by private individuals or they may arise from the pursuit of the interests of various types of collectivities. Intellectuals, when they function as "ideologists", tend to strip such conflicts of their merely interested aspects and to transform them into struggles over eternal truths. They thereby deepen and intensify them. (p. 234)

Abstraction not only polarizes and accentuates differences and conflicts, it can also facilitate the expression of violence. Abstract symbols and categories such as "enemy," "criminal," "communist" can depersonalize or dehumanize the perception of individuals, which may lead to the legitimation and the lowering of inhibitions over the expression of violence (Zimbardo, 1969). Construing individuals in terms of abstract categories can, in a state of violent conflict, also contribute to the activation of the abstract sentiment of contempt, which can augment hostility and lower the degree of guilt over the expression of violence and brutality (Abdennur, 1979).

Therefore, it is suggested that the tendency to avoid polarization, or the tendency towards conflict avoidance, is in harmony with a concrete and pragmatic mode of construing and conceptualizing social conflicts. A concrete conception of conflict as a "problem" achieves, almost automatically, a basic level of consensus as it implies the existence of something dysfunctional that has to be "solved" or "settled" and as such, both parties' efforts are oriented from the beginning in the direction of "solving the problem." But if conflict is conceptualized and presented at the issue level, it becomes difficult to operationalize it into a problem: consensus is likely to be lost as differences become inherent in the context of the whole abstracted and symbolized position. Furthermore, since abstraction leads to the consideration of a problem in the context of the whole position, it results in radicalizing the demands of change or solution and consequently making small compromises unacceptable. An abstract approach tends to increase the polemic nature and intensity of conflict; it also tends to radicalize solutions, thus making the task of problem solving more demanding and challenging. The increase in the degree of conflict and radicalism prompted by abstraction tends to impose high psychological demands on the individual. Therefore, those who are incapable of the challenge will recoil from abstraction in an attempt to recoil from conflict.

Two tests were used to assess the cognitive functioning of subjects:

The Conceptual Systems Test

The *Conceptual Systems Test* (Hoffmeister, 1976) measures the level of conceptual functioning (abstract vs. concrete). This test, a 48-item Likert type of instrument, assigns individuals to one of six levels of conceptual functioning. The levels range from concrete conceptual functioning, which is characterized by a lack of integration of concepts, to abstract functioning, characterized by high integration of concepts.

The CST is a revised version of the I Believe Test (TIB) which has been demonstrated in a considerable number of studies to have high construct and predictive validity (Harvey, 1963, 1964, 1965, 1966, 1967; White and Harvey, 1965; Harvey and Ware, 1967; Ware and Harvey, 1967; Felknor and Harvey, 1970).

The version employed in the present research is the final version (CST 71). It consists of a questionnaire comprising 48 self-statements about the way the subject feels concerning various social and personal issues. The testee is asked to indicate, on a five-point scale, the degree to which he feels that each statement applies to him.

Research has demonstrated that on the basis of their scores, individuals can be assigned to one of two groups (concrete or abstract) with an accuracy of 80 per cent (Hoffmeister, 1976). Assessment of the reliability of the CST has also been favourable: .80 to .90 (Cronbach's coefficient alpha; Hoffmeister, 1976). Volunteers were expected to evidence concrete approaches to interpersonal and social issues.

Defining Issues Test (DIT)

The *Defining Issues Test* (Rest, 1979a) was used to assess the level of abstraction employed in moral thinking. This test measures the relative importance an individual gives to principled and universal moral considerations in evaluating moral dilemmas. The test ranks the moral considerations used according to Kohlberg's (1969) theory of moral development. The most mature, and at the same time most abstract, level of moral thinking corresponds to level six. According to Kohlberg, moral judgement develops in successive stages each of which represents a transformation in the way a person views social interrelationships and social responsibilities. The DIT measures the individual's development by assessing his or her judgement about a number of hypothetical moral dilemmas. It assesses what the individual views as crucial moral issues by presenting him or her with a dilemma and a list of definitions of the major issues involved and then asking him or her to rate the importance of each in deciding what should be done and to rank his or her choices of the four most important issues. The subject's choices of the most important issues are taken as a measure of appreciation of different conceptual frameworks for analyzing moral issues, in other words, of his or her stage of moral reasoning.

Davison and Robbins' (1978) review of several studies of the DIT concludes that the test-retest reliability for this test is generally in the high .70s or .80s. The validity of the test has been demonstrated in studies of longitudinal change which have found that the individual's stage level increases with increasing age (as it should in terms of the theory from which the test derives; see Rest, Davison and Robbins, 1978). It has also been found that the DIT correlates well with other measures of moral reasoning.

4. At the Social-Political Level

At the social-political level the tendency to resolve conflict was measured by the subject's attitude towards political violence. The attitude towards violent political action is seen as an indicator of the degree of acceptance (or tolerance) of direct confrontation (conflict) at the social-political level. The relative acceptance of violent political action implies a readiness or capacity for confrontation and conflict since violent action, when conscious of its objectives as in political action, is the ultimate level of confrontation. Acceptance of violent political action is associated with radicalism and with abstract ideological construction of social issues. Both radicalism and the ideological perspective subordinate liberalism as a process of tolerance, reconciliation, and accommodation of differences.

This variable was measured by a scale that assesses the subject's attitude towards political violence ranging from acceptance to conditional acceptance to absolute rejection. Subjects were asked to respond to three statements designed to depict three types of attitudes towards violent political action: (a) acceptance of violent action as a viable course of action, (b) acceptance of violent political action conditional on the absence of non-violent alternatives, and (c) "absolute" rejection of violent political action as an acceptable course of action. This scale was scored by assigning three points for attitude (a), two points for attitude (b), and one point for attitude (c).

Statement of the Hypotheses

The above described measures of conflict resolution are assumed to be continuous: one end oriented towards conflict or confrontation, the other end oriented towards the avoidance of conflict. Thus, high scores on tests measuring intolerance of ambiguity, preference for articulated forms, abstract functioning, and preference for political violence represent an orientation towards confrontation or conflict. Low scores on these measures represent an opposite tendency, towards the avoidance of conflict.

Based on the previously discussed quality of intervention, correctional volunteers are expected to score lower than non-volunteers on measures of conflict resolution. Social service volunteers are expected to score lower than correctional volunteers on the same measures, that is, further in the direction of conflict avoidance. Non-volunteers are expected to score the highest on these measures, a position at the opposite pole of the continuum. Thus, correctional volunteers (reconcilers) are expected to score somewhere in between non-volunteers (confrontatives) and social service volunteers (avoidants).

The following are the specific hypotheses that were tested in the research:

Hypothesis No. 1
Correctional volunteers will have lower scores than non-volunteers on the following variables:
(a)   Intolerance of ambiguity as measured by Budner's *Intolerance of Ambiguity Scale* (IA).
(b)   Preference for articulated visual forms as measured by figures selected from the *Welsh Figure Preference Test* (WFPT).

(c)   Abstract thinking about social and personal issues as measured by the *Conceptual Systems Test* (CST 71).
(d)   Abstract reasoning in the moral domain as measured by the *Defining Issues Test* (DIT).
(e)   Preference for political violence as measured by the Attitude to Political Violence Scale, developed by the author.

Hypothesis No. 2
Correctional volunteers will have higher scores on the above variables (a, b, c, d, and e) than will social service volunteers.

Hypothesis No. 3
Social service volunteers will have lower scores on the above variables (a, b, c, d, and e) than will non-volunteers.

Seven secondary hypotheses were constructed to compare social service volunteers with non-volunteers on data pertaining to several activities and preferences obtained through a questionnaire. The statements and results of these hypotheses are presented separately towards the end of this chapter as corroborative support to the third hypothesis and to the unity of style postulate.

The Research

The research was conducted in Ottawa, Canada, on groups of university students. University undergraduates, especially those in arts and social sciences, comprise a large proportion of the volunteer population. Although middle-aged, middle-class, and married individuals still represent the largest group of volunteers, undergraduate subjects were preferred for important reasons: the issue of the overall representativeness of the sample was of minor importance because the study was not concerned with demographic and other descriptive characteristics of volunteers. For the purpose of studying the proposed underlying psychological variables, homogeneity was the most important characteristic of the sample. The measures used to assess these variables were sensitive to variations of age, education, professional experience, and the like. The use of an undergraduate sample conveniently solved this problem by maximizing homogeneity. Furthermore, the relatively younger age and shorter period of volunteer experience among undergraduates (as compared with those of adult or elderly volunteers) were seen as an added advantage: these two factors were expected to minimize the chances for the development of elaborate ideological rationalizations concerning volunteering which might interfere with the spontaneity of responses to the measures and questions used. Accordingly, undergraduates who were serving as volunteers in correctional settings were compared with undergraduates who were serving as volunteers in social service agencies and with undergraduates who were not serving as volunteers and who had not assumed volunteer roles previously.

The subjects consisted of undergraduate students enrolled in third and fourth year courses in psychology, sociology, and criminology at the University of Ottawa and Carleton University in Ottawa, Canada, during October, 1981.

The investigator visited eleven classes, briefly introduced the research project, and requested that students complete a number of tests and a questionnaire designed to provide demographic information, information about the individual's volunteering experience, and preferences for certain activities.

In introducing the study the students were told that the research was "a study of university students' participation in social groups designed to yield information about what kinds of students were involved in particular kinds of social activities." They were also told that they "would probably find that completing the tests involved would be an educational experience for students in the social and behavioural sciences." They were asked to complete the questionnaires and tests anonymously and were assured that the confidential nature of their answers would be fully respected.

The students' cooperation was excellent. Almost all students completed the tasks as requested. Only five refused to participate. Twelve questionnaires and test protocols were invalidated because they were incomplete or were completed incorrectly. Five hundred and sixty-eight (568) students completed all tasks in an average of 45 minutes.

Based on the information obtained in the questionnaires, students were either included in the volunteer and non-volunteer research groups or rejected as unsuitable given the working definitions of the study stated in Chapter 1. Accordingly, volunteer groups comprised students who reported that they were currently engaged in some form of volunteer action. Non-volunteers were students who reported that they were not currently nor had they been previously involved in any volunteer activity.

The 568 subjects who completed all test instruments were divided into two groups: volunteers (N = 192) and non-volunteers (N = 376). In accordance with the definition of voluntary action, the volunteer group was refined by discarding students whose "volunteer" activity was motivated either by their interest in obtaining course credits or by their wish to enhance their chances of employment. Subjects belonging to volunteer groups other than those involved in corrections and social service were also eliminated. Moreover, students who volunteered with agencies belonging to the above two groups but whose activity did not involve direct or personal interaction with clients were not included.

The remaining volunteer subjects were divided into two groups: correctional volunteers (N = 48) and social service volunteers (N = 107). Correctional volunteers represented subjects who reported being currently involved in volunteer work with the following agencies: Probation and Aftercare, Parole, Adult Detention Centre, Juvenile Youth Hostel, and Police. Social service volunteers consisted of subjects currently doing volunteer work with the mentally retarded, the physically disabled, and emotionally disturbed children, in hospital, mental health, geriatric, and educational settings.

The non-volunteer group was further refined by eliminating subjects who indicated that they had done volunteer work in the past and those who indicated an intention to volunteer in the near future. The non-volunteer group comprised 170 subjects with no present or past volunteer experience and with no interest in volunteering.

The final research groups consisted of 48 correctional volunteers, 107 social service volunteers, and 170 non-volunteers. Demographic characteristics and the length of volunteer experience of subjects are presented in Table 1 (Appendix).

Statistical analysis of these data revealed that there were no significant differences among the groups in age, marital status, education level, academic status, length of experience as volunteers, or number of hours per week of volunteer work. Slight but statistically significant differences were found in sex ($X^2 = 11.48$, df = 2, $p < .05$). This difference appears to result from the preponderance of females in the social service group.

Apart from the difference in the important factor of sex, the groups were homogeneous in all major characteristics. The sex variable was taken into consideration in the analysis of the results.

Results and Discussion

Unequal Sex Ratios Across Groups

As noted above, there were differences in the sex ratios in the groups, the most pronounced being in the composition of the social service volunteer group. The overall sex difference was statistically significant. A separate analysis of the data was conducted as a result for each of the measures used in the study to determine whether there were any sex differences on any of these measures. No statistically significant differences were found between males and females on any measure, suggesting that sex ratio differences were not confounded with other characteristics of the group in terms of volunteer activity.

The means and standard deviations for each group (non-volunteers, correctional volunteers, and social service volunteers) on each of the measures (*Intolerance of Ambiguity Scale; Form Articulation Test; Conceptual Systems Test; Defining Issues Test*; Attitude to Political Violence Scale) are presented in Table 2 (Appendix). The data were analyzed using the multivariate T-test which is an extension of the T-test and enables one to compare the means of two or more dependent variables at the same time. The scores of social service volunteers and non-volunteers on the personal preference questionnaire were analyzed using Chi square.

Hypothesis 1: Correctional Volunteers Versus Non-Volunteers

It was hypothesized that correctional volunteers would exhibit lower scores on each of the measures than non-volunteers. As hypothesized, the means for the correctional volunteers were lower than for non-volunteers on each of the measures (Table 2, Appendix). An overall multivariate T-test for the five measures revealed a statistically significant difference at the .04 level of significance. However, although the means were all in the expected direction, three out of five were statistically significant: *Intolerance of Ambiguity Scale* ($p < .05$), *Conceptual Systems Test* ($p < .04$), and Attitude to Political Violence Scale ($p < .02$). A summary of statistical analyses is presented in Table 3 (Appendix). In general, the results accord well with the hypothesis that was derived from assumptions about some of the characteristics of correctional volunteers. Taken together, the findings suggest that individuals who are attracted to work in the conciliatory role that is required of the correctional volunteer tend to evidence tendencies towards compromise, concreteness, and political non-confrontativeness.

Hypothesis 2: Correctional Volunteers Versus Social Service Volunteers

It was hypothesized that correctional volunteers would show higher scores on each of the measures than would social service volunteers.

The means for each group on each measure are presented in Table 2 (Appendix). As predicted, the mean for each of the measures is higher for the correctional volunteers than for the social service volunteers. A multivariate T-test revealed a statistical significance at .05. Three measures were statistically significant: *Intolerance of Ambiguity Scale* ($p < .05$), *Form Articulation Scale* ($p < .04$), and Attitude to Political Violence Scale ($p < .02$).

It was hypothesized that correctional volunteers would score higher on measures of conflict resolution (in the direction of confrontation) than social service volunteers. This hypothesis was based on the assumption that the correctional volunteer seeks and gets involved in a conflict situation while the social service volunteer is involved in an essentially non-oppositional role. The overall results support the hypothesis.

Hypothesis 3: Social Service Volunteers Versus Non-Volunteers

It was hypothesized that social service volunteers would show lower scores on each of the measures than non-volunteers. The multivariate T-test indicated that these differences were statistically significant at the $p < .01$ level (Table 5, Appendix). Moreover, four of the five measures were singularly significant: the *Intolerance of Ambiguity Scale* ($p < .01$), the *Defining Issues Test* ($p < .02$), the *Conceptual Systems Test* ($p < .05$), and the Attitude to Political Violence Scale ($p < .01$). This last scale (Attitude to Political Violence) tended to be the measure that best discriminated among the three groups.

These results accord well with the hypothesis derived from the assumption that social service volunteers tend to be individuals who are compromisers, who are concrete in their thinking, and who are likely to avoid oppositional activities and roles.

Conflict Avoidance–Confrontation: A Continuum?

It was assumed that there is a continuum of responsiveness and adaptation to conflict ranging from confrontation at one extreme to avoidance at the other extreme. The results supported the existence of three different positions on the proposed conflict resolution measures. On the confrontation side were non-volunteers, on the avoidance side were social service volunteers, and correctional volunteers were somewhere in between. The three positions might well be continuous. The data tend to suggest a continuum. The three positions might also be spatially distributed, and as such they would constitute more distinct personality orientations. Thus, conflict reconciliation may be more different qualitatively from conflict avoidance and confrontation than initially suspected in the study. Further research can explore these interesting orientations.

Conflict Avoidance: A Personality Style?

Additional support for the view that the conflict avoidance tendency of volunteers would be reflected at various levels of their personality was sought by means of a questionnaire that provided data on their attraction towards and preferences for a variety of activities and experiences. However, only social service volunteers were compared with non-volunteers due to the relatively small size of the correctional volunteer sample and due to the fact that the ultimate concern of the study is with conflict avoidance and its social repercussions. The questionnaire was designed to obtain information for the verification of seven hypotheses. In the interests of economy, the statements, the rationales, and the final results of the hypotheses are presented together.

Theatre

It was hypothesized that social service volunteers would display a higher attraction to live theatre than non-volunteers as measured by (1) interest in theatre, (2) number of plays seen in the past year, (3) interest in theatre as a career, (4) active interest in acting as reflected in experience on stage.

This hypothesis is based on the assumption that theatrical self-expression is essentially an enervated and a compromised form of self-affirmation that is contingent on the acceptance of an audience. On stage, self-affirmation is sought through a role in which the actor poses as somebody else and expresses another person's ideas and opinions. Self-affirmation is compromised in stage acting because it cannot be fully and genuinely realized through make-believe. Moreover, the more genuine and confrontative are modes of self-expression, the less contingent they are on their acceptance by an audience.

The data revealed that a significantly greater number of social service volunteers had a strong interest in live theatre, saw a greater number of plays during the previous year, and had considered acting as a possible career. However, interest, appreciation, and attendance did not correlate with participation. The volunteers' attraction to the theatre appears to be more of a fantasy and subjective inclination than a task-oriented goal. This characteristic in turn may suggest that the theatricism of the social service volunteer is a manifestation of an underlying exhibitionism.

Music

It was hypothesized that among those subjects who indicated a preference for classical music, volunteers would have a greater preference for opera and organ music and less preference for abstract romantic and modern classical music than would non-volunteers.

This hypothesis was based on the assumption that in opera pure instrumental and abstract music is compromised by verbalization and dramatization. Accordingly, it was expected that because of their tendency towards compromise, volunteers would prefer opera to purely abstract classical music.

Volunteers were also expected to prefer organ to piano music because of the low-level tone articulation of the former as contrasted with the highly articulated and circumscribed "crisp" tones of the piano.[2]

The results support the hypothesis. A significantly greater percentage of social service volunteers than non-volunteers preferred

---

[2]During a lecture, a musicologist at the University of Ottawa referred to the piano as a "violent" instrument in the context of commenting on the formality and distinctness of its tones. The vigour and assertiveness of Beethoven's piano sonatas may testify to that claim. The sonatas may well lose this violent quality if played by an organ, flute, or guitar.

opera and organ music (p < .03), while romantic and modern classical music was preferred less by social service volunteers (p < .01).

Favourite Leisure Reading

It was hypothesized that social service volunteers would be *more* interested in poetry and fiction than non-volunteers, and would be *less* interested than non-volunteers in history and general science. This hypothesis is based on the assumption that an individual's favourite leisure reading is a reflection of his basic mental orientation and his fantasy life. On the one hand, poetry and fiction in general involve a compromise between the desire for clarity and objectivity and the freedom to reconstruct or to subjectify reality. Poetry tends to employ concepts in ways that circumvent their precise definitions as this is largely left to the reader's personal interpretation. Science fiction expresses a relevant story in an imaginative context. On the other hand, history and science are constrained by more stringent and reality-bound rules that resist being compromised by subjective reconstruction and modification. The choice of history and science as leisure reading suggests that the reader enjoys and feels at ease with activities that require more disciplined and realistic (confrontative) mental activity.

These hypotheses are also supported by the research. Differences significant at the p < .001 level were found. Approximately 50 per cent of the social service volunteers preferred reading poetry, science fiction, and novels, compared with only 17.5 per cent of non-volunteers.

Films

It was hypothesized that volunteers would prefer musicals and science fiction films to a higher degree than non-volunteers and that volunteers would prefer western and war films to a lesser degree than non-volunteers. This hypothesis is based on the assumption that, whereas musical and science fiction films are designed to dramatize, "musicalize," and cater to the audience's whimsical imagination, western and war films are designed to appear highly realistic. Moreover, they contain a considerable degree of violence. Tolerating or identifying with violent modes of action presupposes a certain capacity for conflict and confrontation.

It was found that a greater percentage of social service volunteers than non-volunteers preferred musicals and science fiction films. Although this difference was in the expected direction, it did not reach statistical significance.

Astrology and Related Activities

It was hypothesized that social service volunteers would indicate an active interest in a larger number of the following than non-volunteers: telepathy, UFOs, astrology, ESP, palmistry, fortune telling, and clairvoyance.

The results supported some of the hypotheses. Although no significant differences were found for ESP, fortune telling, and clairvoyance, a significant number of volunteers indicated an interest in telepathy, UFOs, and astrology. Each of the above fields has both an objective aspect and an unobjectifiable aspect that is either enigmatic or extremely subjective. The compromised approach to reality (subjective vs. objective, obscure vs. clear) provided by these fields is in contrast to rational and scientific confrontation. Such interests may be illustrative of the cognitive patterns of the individual's personality.

Religion

It was hypothesized that when asked about their religious position (atheist, agnostic, theist), volunteers would display less atheistic and agnostic positions than non-volunteers, and that when asked about the intensity of their religious faith, volunteers would indicate a stronger religious faith than non-volunteers. Faith can be viewed as a subjective attempt to humanize, or render tolerable, harsh and ultimately unintelligible human reality. A rational and scientific attitude with respect to ultimate questions implies confronting these questions with reason and science. Thus atheists and, to a lesser extent, agnostics acknowledge and live with the limitations of knowledge rather than compromise the objective perception of reality with the subjective conjectures of faith. The stronger are the subjective conjectures of religious faith, the more significant is the compromise of certain aspects of objective reality.

The Chi square analysis reveals that, as hypothesized, volunteers reported significantly less atheistic and more theistic positions than non-volunteers (p < .02). No significant difference was found with respect to agnosticism. Agnosticism can be seen as a middle position between atheism and theism. In terms of the strength of their religious faith, significant differences were again found between volunteers and non-volunteers when faith was reported to be very strong (p < .03, difference in favour of the volunteers) or to be non-existent (p < .02, difference in favour of non-volunteers).

Teleology

It was hypothesized that social service volunteers would think more frequently than non-volunteers about the following ultimate or teleological questions:

1. What is the purpose of life?
2. What is the good life?
3. What is there after death?

It was assumed that the consideration of the ultimate implication or significance of a certain impulse or drive tends to interfere with the direct and spontaneous expression of that impulse or drive because the drive becomes construed in terms of criteria external to itself. Moral restraints are an example of external criteria dealing with the ultimate social implications of behaviour. Similarly, the basic drive for living (life affirmation) can be subjected to ultimate and teleological questioning or considerations that can interfere with its unity and spontaneity. It is assumed that in a psychologically well-integrated individual "meaning" and "purpose" are inherent in the actual pursuit of existentially meaningful goals which do not require validation from external metaphysical criteria. Teleological considerations may be relevant philosophically. However, on the purely existential level they constitute an interference with the spontaneity of affirmative living, especially when they become a preoccupation. Thus, given the theoretical assumption regarding the non-confrontativeness of volunteers, it was expected that they would evidence more teleological preoccupations than non-volunteers. Teleological questioning tends to arise out of a state of meaninglessness and existential vacuum (Frankl, 1978). This state of meaninglessness is seen here as symptomatic of ambivalent, divided, and weakened life-affirming impulses.

Significant differences in support of the foregoing hypotheses were found in two of the three areas. Volunteers reported frequent thinking about the "purpose of life" (p < .02) and "what is there after death?" (p < .04), significantly more than non-volunteers. The responses of both groups to the question "what is the good life?" suggested that many had misconstrued the question.

In conclusion, the secondary research tended to demonstrate that social service volunteers differ from non-volunteers on a wide range of interests and activities: theatre, music, films, leisure reading, astrology and related interests, strength of religious faith, and concern for ultimate teleological questions. This difference is consistent with a conflict avoidant preference and orientation. These findings accord well with the results obtained by the measures of conflict resolution, thus demonstrating the deep-seated and pervasive tendency towards conflict avoidance that characterizes a certain social group. These findings also lend support to the "unity of style" postulate: a certain mode of conflict resolution (i.e., conflict avoidance) is evidenced at the perceptual, cognitive, and emotional levels of the personality.

Chapter 4

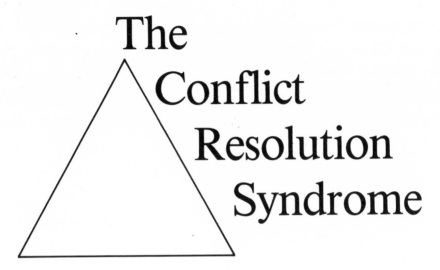

The
Conflict
Resolution
Syndrome

The research described in Chapter 3 reveals that volunteers in social service agencies share a cluster of personality traits, interests, and attitudes that differentiate them from non-volunteers. Clinical observations have been utilized to provide further evidence for the identification of these traits and interests. More than thirty ardent volunteers were interviewed over a period of three years. The interviews sought personal information about attitudes, beliefs, and practices in an informal, friendly, and intimate manner. Some individuals were seen on several occasions. My clinical experience was brought to bear on these interviews, and revelations were systematically recorded. Out of twenty dedicated social service volunteers (both spiritually and socially involved in volunteer work), each with no exception revealed the cluster of traits. Thus, the hypotheses and the confidence with which certain inferences are made from the psychometric data are supported by strong field and clinical evidence that can prove fascinating for any scholar who is motivated to go beyond the surface manifestations of this domain of behaviour.

The analysis indicated that the revealed traits have the common function of avoiding or reducing conflict. Therefore, conflict avoidance becomes an underlying variable responsible for the cluster of traits that will be construed as a "syndrome." This syndrome might most appropriately be termed "the conflict avoidance syndrome"; however, since conflict avoidance is defined as a mode of conflict resolution, and because of the familiarity and widespread use of the latter generic term, the syndrome will be referred to as "The Conflict Resolution Syndrome." This Conflict Resolution Syndrome is not confined to volunteers in social services. There is no reason why it should not describe the same personality orientations of other individuals who may be involved, or have the potential to be involved, in similar social roles and adaptations. All evidence that is presently available points to the universality of this syndrome.

The term "syndrome" carries a connotation of clustering or concomitance of conditions or symptoms, along with a connotation of pathology. On initial thought, the connotation of pathology would seem unjustified in this context, since the traits or dispositions exhibited are socially accepted and none is singularly pathogenic. But the retention of the term "syndrome" is justified by the fact that psychopathological states need not refer only to individual conditions but can also characterize the quality of interpersonal relationships or social adaptations. A certain psychological adaptation may promote a level of stability at the individual personality level; however, the fact of accommodation alone does not ensure the health of that adaptation. The health/pathology status of an adaptation must also be assessed on the basis of its interpersonal and social consequences.

The need to assess the health status of personal adaptations on the basis of criteria beyond their immediate psychological implications can be supported by numerous examples from clinical and organizational behaviour literature. The vast array of sadomasochistic adaptations in families and other intimate attachments where the sadism of one party is accommodated to the masochism of the other are good examples of the inadequacy of using adaptation as the sole criterion for defining mental health. Another example of unhealthy interpersonal adjustments can be seen in the case of "Marital Skew." In this situation, the healthier marital partner, in the interest of minimizing conflict, essentially accepts and supports the frequently bizarre beliefs and behaviour of the spouse (Coleman et al., 1980).

In the area of alcoholism in the family, Whalen (1975) described how certain kinds of women are attracted to the alcoholic man and marry him hoping to find in him an answer to deep unconscious needs of their own. She identified four prototypical women who tend to be involved in such pathological adaptations: (a) the "controller" is the wife with a strong need to control a weakened and dependent person; (b) the "sufferer" has a deep-seated need to suffer; (c) the "waverer" has a poor self-image with fear of being rejected, and therefore the dependency of the alcoholic husband becomes an insurance against abandoning her; and (d) the "punisher" is the wife who hates men and finds the alcoholic husband a convenient target to degrade and emasculate. These adaptations tend to perpetuate the unhealthy attachment and the alcoholism of the husband.

Another example would be the psychological adjustment of an individual with a passive-aggressive personality disorder to a bureaucratic role through which he can create discomfort and misery for others and, at the same time, in which he can protect himself from direct responsibility and exposure. The removal of such an individual from the organizational role that allows the expression of passive-aggression can result in a state of psychological maladjustment and strain. This writer had the opportunity to observe such a case, where the individual concerned developed a severe psychosomatic illness after her transfer from a position that provided her with the opportunity to express her passive-aggression, to another work setting that blocked that opportunity. Thus it can be concluded that certain psychological adjustments that achieve a level of psychological stability may, at the same time, generate a pathological impact on the individual concerned, on others in the interaction setting, and ultimately on society. Certain modes of conflict resolution adaptations depicted in this book are similarly seen as potentially harmful. The social harm such adaptations are likely to engender (further illustrations are presented in the following chapter) has warranted the use of the term "syndrome."

The issue of adaptation is involved in the dilemma that sometimes confronts psychotherapists: should the patient be aided to adjust to the environment regardless of the fact that the environment may be abnormal or unhealthy? Should self-acceptance be encouraged when self-expression is questionable at the moral or social levels? A holistic and integrated assessment of health/ pathology of behaviour must necessarily address two fundamental questions (Coleman et al., 1980): (a) How does the behaviour in question contribute to the health/sickness of the individual? and (b) How does it contribute to the health/pathology of the social or organizational setting, and to the quality of social life in general? It should be added that even at the level of the individual, certain conflict resolution adaptations can present an unhealthy compromise solution. From the perspective of psychodynamics the inability to confront a certain aspect of external or psychological reality tends to lead to a host of psychopathological compromise solutions. Resolutions employing ego defence mechanisms such as reaction formation, denial, compensation, and projection are unhealthy adjustments at the individual level.

An attempt was made to group personality characteristics that expressed conflict avoidance into general traits on the basis of their psychological relatedness or quality. The personality characteristics were obtained by means of (a) psychometric measures, (b) a preference questionnaire, and (c) field or clinical observations. Each trait is substantiated by data from two or three of the above sources. The traits are in some cases presented from a broader perspective in order to show how they become integrated into overall personality expression. Seven traits emerged. Their apparent disconnectedness tends to disappear when the dynamics of psychological adaptation to conflict are closely examined. The consistency and predictability of the seven-trait syndrome were verified by the author's field investigation of groups of volunteers and non-volunteers. Individuals who consistently exhibited role adaptations and sociopolitical attitudes that are typically characterized by conflict avoidance (as defined in this book) tended to evidence the seven traits. Individuals who exhibited the syndrome were found to persist in exhibiting conflict avoidant adaptations and attitudes relative to their level of education and occupation.

The syndrome can be very useful in predicting how an individual will react to or cope with an impending conflict or challenge. The syndrome, as a theoretical construct, can also be used to make predictions about social and political groups through assessing the conflict potential of the personality types that are involved in or are likely to be attracted to the group.

The following are the seven personality traits that have been uncovered and identified as The Conflict Resolution Syndrome. The traits indicate a potential for conflict avoidance, that is, a potential for psychosocial adaptations to (or resolutions of) conflict at the avoidance end of the avoidance-confrontation continuum. The manifestation of these traits, rather than their quality, may be influenced by the sociocultural setting. Later on in this chapter, I shall argue that the syndrome can also represent a personality typology.

1. Non-confrontativeness

The individual recoils from or avoids the various forms of direct confrontation and genuine conflict at both the interpersonal and sociopolitical levels. Violent aggression is most typically avoided. These individuals are more at ease with or prone to utilizing passive-aggressive techniques and strategies. Strong vocal expressiveness or verbal assertiveness that they may sometimes manifest tends to function effectively in low conflict situations. Under serious conflict conditions and danger, this verbal confrontativeness tends to reveal its opposite: a poor ability to cope with stressful crises or conflicts. Thus, a vocal expressive style cannot be taken at face value as part of an overall confrontative style; it may well constitute a compensatory front for an underlying incapacity to cope with strong challenges and conflicts. At the sociopolitical level the individual is neither a conservative, a position that involves strong opposition to change, nor a radical, a position that involves effecting change through confrontative action or violence. He is essentially a compromiser who is likely to follow liberal trends and "in-vogue" causes.

2. Concreteness

The individual evidences a relatively low level of abstract reasoning in construing social problems and political issues. Few abstract principles or comprehensive rationales are utilized when dealing with such matters, since an abstractly held and integrated perspective, as was suggested earlier, is conducive to confrontation and conflict. The individual's approach is basically one of problem-solving characterized by appeasement and conflict reduction, an approach that is devoid of an ideological perspective, that is, an integrated *a priori* system of concepts and principles.

A concrete pragmatic approach tends to coexist with universalized, spiritualized, and absolutely held notions. For example, the type of socialism that sometimes may be advocated does not involve a radical rejection of the existing social order in favour of a revolutionary vision of a new social order; rather it is a product of moral enthusiasm for absolutely held notions of love, equality, and peace. These absolute notions usually lack intellectual differentiation and integration and are, therefore, amenable to arbitrary operationalization and compromise.

3. Theatricism and Latent Exhibitionism

The individual shows a fascination with live theatre and a desire (actually carried out or fantasized) to act. This attraction to the theatre may be a manifestation of a more general and pervasive personality tendency towards self-presentation and self-assertion through exhibition. Exhibitionism tends to presuppose an audience that is either immediately present, or permanently incorporated within the individual's self. Motivated by the desire to win the approval of the audience, the subject suppresses his or her own thoughts and actions and displays the kind of behaviour that appeals to the audience. Thus, exhibitionistic assertive behaviour is compromised at its inception by the desire to please the audience. Also, theatrical expression is compromised at the level of performance, where the actor confronts the audience from behind the fictitious mask of the role.[3] Direct forms of self-assertion have the self as the main delineator and reference for action. Ideology, or integrated beliefs and principles, when incorporated within the self, become aspects of the self and not the audience. Accordingly, they are avoided by the individual due to their strong conflict potential, in favour of less challenging exhibitionistic and fragmented notions.

4. Verbalism

The individual exhibits excessive reliance on the medium of language in certain aspects of the presentation of self and in recreational activities.

---

[3]A famous actor, Henry Fonda, stated that while he has no problem playing any role, he tends to feel tense whenever he introduces members of his show to the audience. His explanation of this paradox is that he feels secure while acting for he "hides behind the role." However, introducing the cast implies confronting the audience directly: without a role and on more objective (non-fictitious) grounds.

A concept tends to have certain specific or recognizable denotations. The clearer and the more unequivocal the denotation is, the clearer is the concept. Words can be used in contexts (metaphorical, for example) where their denotation is expanded, rendered less precise and consequently more amenable to subjective interpretations. This process tends to flatter the narcissistic aspect of the personality, particularly the sense of omnipotence. The subject can "impart" or "create" meaning largely by the manipulation of linguistic concepts, as in the case of "abstract" poetry.

A similar semantic indulgence can be achieved by brooding over and preaching about certain religious concepts that do not possess tangible denotations such as the Holy Spirit, grace, angels, deities, and so on. Such metaphorical concepts allow the subject the freedom to dwell on them while protected from the infringements of distinct objective denotations or scientific definitions. The subjective, spiritual, moral, and aesthetic contexts where this activity takes place often discourage the demands for precision and clarity. Scientific fields thwart this type of verbal indulgence, but the conflict avoidant personality type tends to maintain it despite a career in science or technology.[4]

A very strong correlation was found among the indicators of theatricism, interest in poetry, and teleological concerns. This association is not surprising, since it can be readily observed that stage and words are part and parcel of religious public expression and communication.

5. A Need for Absolutes

The individual holds certain concepts and moral positions as absolutes. The absolute status of these concepts and positions is usually anchored to a religious faith that also invites several metaphysical assumptions, which are based on faith rather than on reason. In cases where a crystallized religious faith is absent, the individual

---

[4]Hervey Cleckley (1976) in *The Mask of Sanity* marvelled at how certain individuals "reverently acclaim as the superlative expression of genius James Joyce's *Finnegans Wake*, a 628-page collection of erudite gibberish indistinguishable to most people from the familiar word salad produced by hebephrenic patients on the back wards of any state hospital" (p. 7). The experience of dwelling upon the semantic and conceptual "muddle" presented in works such as *Finnegans Wake* is seen as a quest for "meaning" for those who indulge in it; however, it seems more of an affective experience than meaning in the generally understood sense of the word, that is, meaning as denotation.

holds as absolutely true or good certain moral universals, such as equality, love, humanitarian charity, peace, repudiation of violence, and the like. The individual employs reason to defend and justify such absolutely held concepts, but seldom does he use it as a critical tool that can modify and adapt their meaning to the demands of new information and different social conditions.

An absolute concept is distinguishable from an abstract one. An absolute concept is held without any recognition of relative values. Its meaning is largely self-contained and, therefore, independent of the context of other concepts. For example, love and peace can be held as absolutely good regardless of temporal and contextual changes that are capable of making love and peace dysfunctional and harmful to a social system.

In the case of the abstract concept, the meaning is, to a certain extent, dependent upon other concepts that constitute the intellectual context in which it is utilized. The practical meaning of the abstractly used concept is determined not only by its connotations, but also by its denotations in the particular context where it is utilized. For example, concepts such as social class or freedom are not confined to their nineteenth-century definitions, but their definitions are, to a certain extent, altered to suit the intellectual and social setting they are intended to explain.

There appears to be a similarity between absolute and concrete concepts. In both cases, the perception of and attitude towards the concept are relatively independent of the larger context in which it inheres and which should have a certain impact on its meaning. For example, a concrete perception of justice as legality confines the concept of justice to the concrete legal outcome regardless of the broader context of the concept. This may explain why extreme concreteness tends to coexist with absolutely held concepts and notions.[5]

The capacity of an abstract concept to integrate its connotations with its changing denotations renders it more confrontative and conflict-laden than an absolute or a concrete concept. For example, the absolute concepts of religion tend to acquire the confrontative qualities of abstract concepts when they become part of a reli-

---

[5]Goldstein (1940) noted that schizophrenic thinking shifts between extreme concreteness and extreme globality. In the present study subjects in the CST concrete category had significantly high teleological concerns.

gious dogma, that is, when they are integrated into a system of abstract religious principles and notions.

It can be argued that a capacity for confrontation promotes an abstract sociopolitical perspective, whereas a tendency towards conflict avoidance promotes a concrete perspective. Therefore, by utilizing absolute and/or concrete concepts, the individual manages to avoid a radical confrontation with conflict.

Education, intellectual skills, and the exposure to critical thinking are cognitive variables that can enhance the individual's ability to abstract and consequently increase the level of conflict. However, it is the latent capacity for confrontation in the individual that determines the extent of his or her radicalism. Intellectual sophistication can influence social vision and coping style, but it can hardly make someone more radical than he or she is actually capable of being.

6. An Interest in Compromised Reality

The individual is likely to exhibit an interest in or even a fascination with enigmatic or pseudo-scientific fields such as telepathy, astrology, and various mystical, occult, and religious ideas which are a mixture of fact and absurdity. A high degree of affective investment in science fiction and similar forms of fantasy can also be observed. Such fields usually constitute enjoyable preoccupations rather than instrumental disciplines for extending scientific or philosophical knowledge. They are free of the constraints of objective and scientific procedures. They allow the imagination to roam freely and enable the individual to enjoy a magical or theatrical control of reality. This interest in enigma and the absurd should be distinguished from the activity, expressed in creative fantasy or in literary and artistic constructions of reality, that enhances people's perspective on life issues and may, in fact, inspire scientific discoveries. The former interest is in the service of narcissism where an intellectual "muddle" is actively sought after and enjoyed. This interest in intellectual and verbal muddles is the opposite of the drive towards clarity in communication and parsimony of expression; it precludes the formation of finite and clearly circumscribed concepts and relationships which directly converge on reality demanding confrontation with it. Enigma, the absurd, and denotative ambiguity all can temporarily shield the ego from confronting a threatening, finite, and alien world.[6]

7. Teleological Preoccupations

These individuals are likely to have strong interests or preoccupations with what appear to be fundamental teleological questions. However, their teleological preoccupations represent more than asking and attempting to answer ultimate questions. In fact, they are only pseudo-questions and subjective preoccupations that do not aim for clear or objective answers. Answers to questions about the purpose of life, or what is after death, if they are ever to be answered, can only come from the growth of knowledge about the biological and chemical nature of life and the universe. But these individuals seldom seek answers to their teleological concerns in the realm of science. On the contrary, they seek answers at the moral and at the absolute religious levels which serve subjective needs rather than objective truth.

Teleological preoccupations imply a level of interference with the spontaneity of the life-affirming impulse because they constitute a level of hesitancy and doubt, or ambivalence, in the drive or will to live. A social act may have a moral purpose; however, there is no objective indication that the existence of the human species has any moral purpose. In physically and psychologically healthy individuals the impulse for living is spontaneous and life-affirming, and it does not need to be validated by external crite-

---

[6]A paper entitled "In Pursuit of the Conceptual Muddle: the Teaching of Humanities in the Light of Psychopathology" was delivered by this author at a Graduates' Forum, University of Ottawa, 1985. The paper depicted the interest in absurd literary expression as a cognitive preoccupation that is ultimately in the service of narcissism. The attraction to the conceptual muddle is seen by the author as the opposite of the drive for clarity, simplicity, and parsimony which characterizes the scientific approach. This preoccupation with the absurd verbal expression affords a certain protection to the narcissistically laden ego from the threatening experience of the finite which tends to promote the consciousness of the "limit": limits of one's talents and opportunities. The impact of scientific consciousness on personality usually promotes modesty, while the cultivation of the consciousness of the muddle tends to promote vanity, absent-mindedness, and exhibitionism. The psychopathological involvement of the latter in education can result from the enthusiastic "teaching" of literary works belonging to writers such as Kafka, Joyce, and Beckett at the college level. The acquisition of this style of expression and thinking by students with borderline and schizoid personality organizations can aggravate their already weakened ties with reality.

ria.[7] The fact of being born and living needs no proof or reason to justify it.[8] The stronger and more persistent teleological preoccupations are, the higher is the degree of ambivalence at the level of the will. Teleological views can be endorsed without constituting an individual preoccupation. This can take place when an individual is fully integrated in a cohesive social group. In this case, the collectively held religious belief encourages certain forms of confrontation.

Thus the asking and answering of ultimate questions remains an essentially individualized subjective (narcissistic) preoccupation which compromises the life-affirming impulses and promotes otherworldly concerns. Often the decision to volunteer is sought as an answer to the question of what is the purpose of life. "We are here to do good" is the answer. The nature of this moral resolution itself raises a new question: why is it that the objects of the good deed are often individuals who, despite the helping intervention, cannot be reinstated into the ranks of the healthy and fully living?

The Conflict Resolution Syndrome in Perspective

An individual's typical mode of reacting to or dealing with conflict involves his total personality organization, which includes his neurophysiological organization. When all of the above conflict resolution traits cluster in an individual's personality, the syndrome indicates a weak ego. Ego strength is here defined as the capacity to face and cope effectively with strong conflicts and challenges at most major levels of behaviour: the reflexive, emotive, perceptual, conceptual, interpretive, and expressive levels.

The syndrome may also be viewed as indicating a weak ego when ego strength is seen in terms of reality relations. Freud (1927) stated that in order to achieve mental and emotional maturity, man must give up infantile and narcissistic constructions of reality and merge into a "hostile world" where one can rely only on objectiv-

---

[7]In a letter to Princess Bonaparte, Freud (1961) wrote: "The moment one inquires about the sense or value of life, one is sick."

[8]A certain familiar hymn proclaims that after finding Jesus "I have found a reason to go on." The implication is that one needs a "reason" to go on living. But this "reason" is a form of metaphysical validation or purpose and not a purpose in the existential (logotherapeutic) sense described by Viktor Frankl in his book *Man's Search for Meaning* (1968).

ity to confront harsh reality. Individuals who exhibit the above Conflict Resolution Syndrome appear to resist a total acceptance of hostile reality despite high levels of intelligence and education. Concessions to objectivity and scientific approaches among these individuals are often segmented or counterbalanced by indulgences in absolute thinking and in religious and teleological beliefs. These beliefs are maintained despite the lack of objective evidence, and this may lead to weakened ties with certain aspects of reality. For example, absolute and metaphysical concepts, unlike scientific ones, connect loosely to the objective world because their denotations are either unclear or difficult to operationalize.[9]

Conflict Resolution and Other Typologies

The Conflict Resolution Syndrome can be treated as an indicator of a personality typology that is often easy to discern from attitudes towards conflict and ways of dealing with conflict. Preliminary research indicates that the typology extends beyond social service volunteers to other social groups.

This typology is similar, at least at a rudimentary level, to that described by Jaensch (1938) in his book *Der Gegentypus*.[10] In this book Jaensch postulated the unity of style of an individual and reported the discovery of a consistent human type he called the "Anti-Type." Jaensch conducted some experiments in perception and found the Anti-Type to be typically synaesthetic. Synaesthesia is the propensity in some individuals to experience concomitance in sensation; that is, they experience sensations from a sense other than the one being stimulated, as in colour-hearing and tone-seeing. For Jaensch, this was a manifestation of perceptual slovenliness, where the qualities of one sense are carelessly mixed with those of another. In other perceptual tasks Jaensch found the Anti-Type to be characterized by ambiguous and indefinite judgements and to be lacking in perseverance. He argued that the Anti-Type's "subjective and unstable" evaluation of sensory stimuli carries over

---

[9]Schizoid and borderline personality disorders that are characterized by weak ego integration, narcissism, and magical thinking (American Psychiatric Association, DSM III, 1979) tend to exhibit most of the traits of the Conflict Resolution Syndrome. The converse, however, is not true.

[10]The contents of this book, which has not yet been translated into English, were described briefly by Frenkel-Brunswik (1949, 1954).

into a general lack of firmness and stability in his personality. He suggested that "liberalism" of every kind, and "adaptability" in general, are associated with lack of strong ties with reality, and with general flaccidity and weak integration. "The Anti-Type has no firm tie with reality. He is the liberalist at large . . . . This social liberalism is paralleled by innumerable other forms of liberalism, all of them mentally rooted in the Anti-Type: liberalism of knowledge, of perception, of art, etc." (quoted in Frenkel-Brunswik, 1954, p. 253). Jaensch assumed this type to be degenerative, morbid, and dangerous to society. Rigid control, perseverance, and integration of differences are the major characteristics of the "J-Type," which Jaensch considered to be the opposite of the "Anti-Type." The "J-Type" personifies discipline.

Frenkel-Brunswik, who identified another personality type, the "Authoritarian Personality" (Adorno et al., 1950), suggested that "It is time to bring the relevance of Jaensch to our problem . . . . Except for the fact of its glorification by Jaensch, this ideal (J-Type) shows striking structural similarities to our conceptualization of the authoritarian personality which thus receives support from a source certainly not biased in our direction." (1954, p. 227)

The two broad typologies, Jaensch's J-Type and Adorno's "Authoritarian Personality," are essentially similar; their difference stems mainly from the authors' contrasting ideological evaluations of the social value of the personality characteristics that the types subsumed. It appears that Adorno's conceptualization of the authoritarian personality was inspired by Jaensch's formulation of the J-Type but subjected to a radical inversion of value perspective. Whereas Jaensch saw the J-Type as the ideal, Adorno was highly opposed to the authoritarian personality, which he saw as its equivalent. In fact, he relabelled the characteristics of Jaensch's ideal type (discipline, perseverance, and integration) as rigidity, dogmatism, conventionalism, and intolerance of ambiguity. Conversely, the traits of the Anti-Type which Jaensch evaluated negatively (instability, attitudinal flaccidity, generalized liberalism) Adorno referred to as flexibility, adaptability, and tolerance: democratic ideals.

Such dramatic inversion of value perspective is reminiscent of the radical "inversion of values" effected by the founders of the Christian religion two millennia ago, as analyzed by Nietzsche in his *On the Genealogy of Morals* (1887). According to Nietzsche, the Roman aristocratic ideals of strength, abundance, and honour were radically inverted into the "blessed are the meek" ideal.

Although the psychological subject matter may be the same, the utilization of value-laden concepts (rigidity, dogmatism, flexibility, etc.) can significantly distort the psychological reality in question. The use of such value-laden constructs in *The Authoritarian Personality* (Adorno et al., 1950) has undermined its scientific merit. These constructs also tended to block the investigation of many important variables. The fascination with the study of rigidity-flexibility, potential fascism, and the F-scale did not allow the investigation to go beyond the study of sociopolitical attitudes to a consideration of other variables such as cognitive complexity, level of abstraction, and the degree of integration of political attitudes. These latter traits, because they are general style elements, may be more predictive of behaviour than is attitude. The study of attitudes may be useful for predicting voting patterns, but not for predicting how individuals with the same political views may react to political conflicts or crises.

Rokeach (1960) in his *The Open and Closed Mind* tried to move away from researchers' preoccupation with right wing politics; he regarded dogmatism as characteristic of an individual's cognitive structure and not tied to a specific ideology. However, his conceptualization was still biased in the direction of psychodynamics and the conceptual framework of the Authoritarian Personality research. It may well be that psychodynamic variables are only superficial ones when compared to more formal style elements. A "closed" or an "open" mind need not be only a function of a reaction to anxiety arising from ambiguity or fear of change, but ultimately may be a characteristic that is dictated by basic thinking modes (e.g., abstract/concrete) and generalized personality elements such as the capacity for conflict. For example, the abstract deductive way of thinking tends to be deterministic, categorical, discriminatory, "closed," and oriented towards all-encompassing perspectives such as ideology in political thinking. In contrast, a concrete and pragmatic mode of thinking tends to be atomistic, less integrated, and hence "open" to negotiation and compromise.

Goldstein (1940) tried to show, on the basis of data on brain-damaged individuals, that an abstract approach characterizes psychologically and neurologically healthy individuals who confront reality in an "active" manner. The concrete approach, according to Goldstein, is essentially "passive," since its main concern is with adaptation. He also demonstrated that concreteness increases with the severity of brain damage and in simple schizophrenia. These two basic cognitive styles, abstract and concrete, along with cognitive complexity and intelligence, may, under certain conditions, be better predictors of dogmatic behaviour than psychodynamic variables such as the management of anxiety and ego defence mechanisms. To limit the researcher's perspective to psychodynamics and to treat psychodynamic variables as *the* independent variables would be to distort the real picture in this area of personality functioning. The conceptualization and study presented in this book suggest that the tendency towards conflict or conflict avoidance as a personality style element may, if adequately measured, constitute a good predictor of several forms of behaviour including compromise, opposition, radicalism, and some aspects of authoritarianism.

A more fruitful strategy for further researching such typologies would be: first, to define and employ concepts in a value-free manner that minimizes the impact of their moral and political connotations; second, to study individual differences in fundamental psychological functioning such as perceptual, cognitive, and neuropsychological processes in socially and politically neutral settings. Witkin's (1962) field dependent/independent typology was developed under such proper scientific approaches; however, its growth was eventually thwarted due to the inability of researchers to go beyond the two dimensions of field dependent/independent and the two dimensions of their generalized personality correlates of leveller/sharpener. Third, general style elements that can consistently link neurophysiological, genetic, psychodynamic, and sociopolitical variables should be sought and verified. Such "formal style elements," as Frenkel-Brunswik (1949) calls them, are more meaningfully predictive of behaviour than "content" variables pertaining, for example, to sex or hostility. The Conflict Resolution Syndrome presented in this book attempts to achieve such linking among divergent variables at different levels of personality functioning. The next chapter further illustrates the dynamics of conflict resolution in the psychological, social, and political functioning of volunteers.

Chapter 5

Volunteers, Volunteerism, and Society

The research and analysis presented in the previous chapters attempted to demonstrate that certain roles can be characterized as demanding a certain mode of conflict resolution, and that these modes of conflict resolution can exist as personality variables capable of motivating an individual to choose and adjust to a specific role. In adjusting to the chosen role, the personality tends to be dynamically, not passively, influenced by that role. The individual, on the other hand, can modify the role or organization according to elements inherent in his or her personality (Fromm, 1941, 1955), despite the fact that organizational structures tend to resist modification by individual members. These structures and their functions may, therefore, be significantly influenced by the styles of individuals who dominate or control them. This type of individual impact on the organization is more likely to take place in social and political agencies than in industrial ones. Thus, the domination and control of certain social agencies by conflict avoidant personality types are likely to influence ideological and political trends in a society.

It should be stressed in this context that individual or group behaviour that appears to be compatible with popular moral notions or tends to achieve a certain social adjustment within a sociocultural setting need not be automatically awarded a clean bill of psychological and social health. Conscientious objectors may be peace-loving, but their neurological normality and other dimensions of their mental or physical health should be established on other than moral grounds, as is hinted by Nassi and Abramowitz (1976). An electroencephalographic study found conscientious objectors to evidence more EEG abnormalities than a group of incarcerated psychopaths.

Traditional Volunteerism

In order to comprehend the social implications of the new volunteerism movement, it is important to identify the main features of traditional volunteerism at the theological, philosophical, social, emotional, and practical levels.

1. Theological Level

The act of giving charitable help to the needy is usually seen as an act that is good in itself. The belief in the intrinsic goodness of the charitable act seems to be based on four assumptions:
(a)   Goodness is equated with "good intention" (as opposed to bad or "evil intention"), rather than with the act itself.
(b)   The charitable act is a religious duty: it is simultaneously both a divine and a communal command.
(c)   As a unit of behaviour the charitable act is capable of earning the rewards of grace and salvation in the eyes of God.
(d)   Not only do some people need help, but a number of people need *to* help.
Thus the charitable act is perceived as good for God, good for the recipient, good for the doer, and good for society. This amounts to an absolutist attitude towards the goodness of charity.

2. Philosophical-Social Level

There are at least three assumptions that constitute the principles of traditional volunteerism:
(a)   It is assumed that helping some individuals will contribute to helping society as a whole. Simply stated, the greater the number of individuals who are helped, the better it is for every-

body. The utilitarian maxim of J. S. Mill, "the greatest good for the greatest number," is an implicit principle of classical volunteerism.

(b)   The effect of helping is considered to be cumulative; any effort at helping is better than no effort at all: "Do what you can . . . where you can . . . with what you have."

(c)   It is assumed that "good" action cannot have negative effects; good is good.

All of the above assumptions naively adopt a continuum conception regarding the effect of social action. This conception denies the possibility of dialectical changes through time and from quantity to quality. Assumption (a) applies to an atomistic perception that society is equivalent to the sum of its parts rather than to an organic union of conflicting groups and classes. Assumption (b) excludes the possibility that a decision not to act can be a positive decision. When a good act runs the risk of being harmful or insignificant, then non-action can have a positive value. "I prefer a strong evil to a small good," said St. Augustine, an aphorism that acknowledges dialectics in social interactions. Assumption (c) excludes the possibility that intimate personal interaction can result in harmful consequences to the parties involved despite good intentions, that, as the common saying puts it, "the road to hell is paved with good intentions."

3. Emotional Level

One of the most salient characteristics of the traditional volunteer is "enthusiasm" or "zeal." The enthusiasm motivating the volunteer to act can be distinguished from the type of motivation for action found in ideologically committed individuals. The ideologically rooted intention to act has a deductive quality; the motivation to act "flows" from, or seeks to express and translate into action, the *a priori* concepts and abstract principles of the individual's ideology or dogma. In contrast, the enthusiasm of middle-class traditional volunteerism tends to centre on practical action and keep the relevant intellectual justifications in abeyance. The traditional volunteer's enthusiasm for "doing something about the problem" has a compulsive quality that serves to displace *a priori* intellectual considerations. Instead of these, some general moral platitudes are repeated to justify the action. One could argue that volunteerism is characterized by "enthusiasm in lieu of intellect."

In this context, Henry C. Link's (1936) remarkable book, *The Return to Religion*, a best-seller from 1936 to 1941, is worth noting. The author, a consulting psychologist for a business corporation, and a former atheist, reported that he regained his lost enthusiasm for life by a return to religion. In recalling his return to mental health and in advising others to follow his lead, he advocated the rejection of traditional therapeutic approaches that require withdrawal, self-examination, and reflection. These, he argued, are selfish and bad. Instead of the Socratic maxim "Know thyself," Link recommended, "Behave yourself," because "a good personality or character is achieved by practice, not by introspection." He argued that extroversion, not introversion, was required. He suggested that extroversion, which involves sociability, amiability, and service to others, is unselfish and good. He considered that one of the main functions of religion is to discipline the personality by developing extroversion. Religion, he asserted, is "an aggressive mode of life by which the individual becomes the master of his environment, not its complacent victim." Religion was assumed to be an incentive, a stimulant, a propellant to enthusiasm and action which would combat apathy and depression. Jesus was the great extrovert. Later in this chapter, the role of enthusiasm in the volunteer movement will be further discussed.

4. Practical Level: a Legacy of Common Sense

In traditional volunteerism the concern is with a particular individual or group with a problem. The problematic situation is identified at a concrete level and practical help is prescribed. The helping intervention ignores the social structure both as a cause of the problem and as an approach to solving it. The perspective is individualistic and atomistic rather than social or global.

A critical analysis of the ideological notions assumed by traditional volunteerism readily reveals erroneous sociological presuppositions and a lack of any in-depth philosophical questioning of notions. Volunteerism does not possess a coherent ideology, at least in terms of a unified system of *thought* or a set of intellectually integrated concepts and principles that provide an explanation for the problem it seeks to solve and a justification for the line of intervention followed. But even though traditional volunteerism does not qualify as a coherent system of thought, this does not mean that, as a system of action, it is disjointed and haphazard. On the contrary, close examination reveals that volunteerism is an integrated system of *action* that is well anchored in certain religious-cultural traditions, and in the ranks of the upper middle class, the interests of which it ultimately serves.

The apparently disjointed notions and clichés traditional volunteerism proclaims tend to serve specific practical purposes that are functional for the maintenance of volunteerism as a movement. The notions are *not* intended to aspire to the status of a dogma or an ideology. An ideology involves constant interpretation, evaluation, and rationalization of action, intellectual activities that tend to be dysfunctional to the movement because of the conflict potential of abstraction. It should be added that the notions of volunteerism do not represent a "false consciousness," that is, a misguided and practically irrelevant mental representation of reality. They represent a false consciousness only in that they are rationalizations and not critically and clearly thought-out principles. However, as rationalizations of action, they are a functional and an integral part of the movement.

The functional, dynamic relationship between the notions and the practice of volunteerism reveals a great deal about the psychosocial nature of this movement. For example, the matter-of-fact acceptance of the intrinsic goodness of the charitable act promotes an attitude that discourages the questioning of its actual implications. Any questioning or analysis of the social implications of the charitable act endangers its credibility in the eyes of the volunteer and the general public. A second example is the adoption of the commonsensical notion that charity has a cumulative good effect on society as a whole. This serves to maintain a positive attitude towards volunteering among the ranks of volunteers. Accordingly, even in cases where voluntary acts are ineffective, the acts can be rationalized as being good for society because of the presumed cumulative effects of good intentions.

A third example of the integrated approach of traditional volunteerism is the concrete pragmatic construing of social problems. By adopting a pragmatic approach to social problems, individuals and groups can minimize the disagreement and contradiction that may arise from seeking a more abstract and comprehensive understanding of the problem. The more abstract an issue is made, the greater is the degree of disagreement that is likely to ensue. However, even when pragmatic approaches are adopted, people may still disagree on the means of carrying out a certain action, particularly when they have personal vested interests in its outcome. But in the case of volunteer activity, personal profits or interests are often minimal, and hence disagreement on the means is expected to be minimal. Therefore, in the case of volunteer action, concreteness, most typically, tends to foster consensus. It should be noted that moral and religious notions such as love, equality, sin, and the like do not constitute abstract concepts that are connected to action as in the case of ideological concepts; they usually are blanket platitudes that actually protect and foster concrete strategies of intervention. In this concrete approach, a commonsensical equation that can explain both success and failure tends to prevail: if the problematic condition is ameliorated as a result of the helping intervention, then this is a demonstration of the usefulness of such intervention; if no improvement is noticed, then this is an indication that more volunteer help is needed.

The functional aspect of volunteer notions can also be depicted at the affective level. As noted earlier, the dominant sentiment associated with volunteering activity is enthusiasm for involvement and action. This type of enthusiasm has an almost compulsive quality in its preoccupation with action. It can be viewed as serving two functions: (a) a defensive reaction against the indulgence in intellectual speculation and analysis of action; (b) an enhancement of *esprit de corps* and group cohesiveness. Cohesiveness tends to counteract the disruptive influence of inside critics who might challenge the group's established norms (Schachter, 1968).

Thus, close examination of the notions and strategies of traditional volunteerism reveals that they are both aspects of a certain integrated approach. The foregoing analysis indicates that volunteer notions and strategies have as a major goal the denial, the bypassing, and the subordination of critical thinking with respect to social problems. This allegiance to common sense and the repudiation of critical thought seem to have remained a characteristic of traditional volunteerism.

Traditional volunteerism proclaiming the Christian ethic of charity tends to recruit individuals with the conflict avoidant personality type which is highly adaptive to an altruistic helping role and the volunteer movement in general. The movement operates within a sociopolitical system that tolerates its activities and finds them geared to its advantage. The folkish commonsensical approach that evolved basically among female church volunteers was one of the reasons the movement was well accommodated within the political system. A movement embracing the teachings of Jeremy Bentham—which Karl Marx described as "homespun common sense"—poses little threat to the status quo.

Traditional volunteerism is also firmly anchored in the anti-intellectual and pro-commonsense tradition that reached its highest expressions among business circles and in the writing of self-made industrialists after the middle of the nineteenth century. Richard Hofstadter (1966) in his "Anti-intellectualism in American Life" maintains that American anti-intellectualism can be broadly interpreted:

> as a suspicion of intellect itself, it is part of the extensive American devotion to practicality and direct experience which ramifies through almost every area of American Life. With some variations of details suitable to social classes and historical circumstances, the excessive practical bias so often attributed only to business is found almost everywhere in America . . . . Practical Vigor is a virtue; what has been spiritually crippling in our history is the tendency to make a mystique of practicality. (pp. 236-237)

When such a movement develops, it acquires tradition, social character, and autonomy, all of which tend to resist extinction. The main threats against volunteering as a movement came from the professionalization of the social service system and from the development of political ideologies such as socialism, Marxism, and Fascism which have comprehensive or sophisticated theories of society. Both tended to rob volunteerism of its credibility. The folkish common sense that mobilized church groups towards charity became inadequate as dedicated volunteers became involved with governmental social agencies and large publicly funded volunteer organizations. However, common sense was not given up in favour of social science thinking by the active ranks of service-oriented volunteers. Rather, a "manipulative" strategy was adopted to operate on behalf of and in defence of common sense, a strategy of ignoring and dodging conceptual and theoretical analysis in social problems. This strategy culminated in the early phase of new volunteerism.

New Volunteerism

The reawakening and proliferation of volunteerism in the last two and a half decades have engendered certain modifications in the rationale and modes of operation of traditional volunteerism. However, it can still be stated that new volunteerism is firmly rooted in the approaches of traditional volunteerism. In the quality of the literature being published, and in the orientation of programs, one can readily discern a continuity and consistency in the volunteering tradition.[11] This continuity can be explained as resulting from the persistence of the structure of liberalism and the Christian ethic of charity, which tend to recruit individuals with personalities attracted to and suited for the volunteer role. The social quality of a role (role structure) and the psychological quality of the interaction it involves can be maintained despite changes in the content and location of the role. For example, the role structure and quality of interaction of a classical missionary working in the relief of certain afflicted African natives are very similar to those of a dedicated volunteer working in a modern institution for the mentally retarded. The two volunteers engage in the same type of power relationship with their clients, and both are regularly exposed to helplessness, misery and bad odours.

---

[11]During the last seven years the writer has been examining the current literature on social service volunteering. A large number of pamphlets, reports, program descriptions and evaluations, conferences, and books on the subject have been critically examined. A large amount of intellectually impoverished common sense has been produced, indicating the persistence of the spirit and personality style of traditional volunteers.

The impoverishment of the general literature seems to a certain extent balanced by the emergence of related academic journals such as the *Journal of Community Action* and the *Journal of Voluntary Action Research*. The latter has been published since 1972 by the Association of Voluntary Action Scholars (AVAS), with headquarters at Pennsylvania State University. Articles meeting standard academic criteria deal with diversified topics pertaining to volunteering. However, the utilization of standard research methodology does not guarantee an adequate scientific approach to the problem addressed. The identification and definition of any "social problem," as well as the proposed solutions to it, involve not only matters of fact and theory but also matters of value. It is incumbent on the social scientist playing the role of advocate to adopt a comprehensive view that makes explicit the value assumptions of the approach, the ultimate social effects of the approach or intervention (as distinguished from the immediate or short-term results), and the value implications of these long-term policies. Adequate program evaluation and research must take all three factors into account (cf. Doris, 1982).

Despite the incorporation of social science concepts and methods, the anti-intellectual commonsensical approach is still maintained. This is largely achieved through the adoption of concrete pragmatic approaches that dodge conflict with social science theories. The techniques of social sciences are embraced (e.g., counselling, crisis intervention, rehabilitation, specialized evaluation, and therapeutic skills), but social science as social theory or as an analysis of the quality of social life is situationally fragmented or displaced by popular assumptions.

Instead of the altruistic and religious notions of traditional volunteerism, new volunteerism acknowledges self-interest as the basic motive in volunteering, thereby conceding to social science theory and to the psychoanalytic notion that all that the ego seeks is self-serving. This head-on acknowledgement helps new volunteerism escape the intimidating accusations of hidden motives posed from a psychoanalytic perspective, and at the same time converts this self-interest into an inducement for and promotion of volunteering. Thus, "opportunity for personal growth," "development of new skills," "meeting new people," "having fun," and so on, are advertised as rewards for volunteering. This amounts to the promotion of purely individualistic motives. The appeal to individualistic, personal motives for a supposedly socially concerned activity goes beyond the atomistic approach of classical volunteerism and allies itself with the narcissistic orientations of the contemporary "Culture of Narcissism" described by Christopher Lasch (1979). The self-centred, narcissistic aspect of volunteering is reflected in the following quotation by Miller (1974b):

> But the greatest gain of all is the psychic income to every individual volunteer who increases his sense of dignity and identity and knows that he is often in a one-to-one relationship supplying an intangible need that cannot be paid for—even if money were available. (p. 191)

A traditional tenet that is maintained in new volunteerism is that of individual and private intervention. This ideological maxim proclaims that an effort on the individual level will pull the country out of crisis situations. Eriksson-Joslyn (1973-74) summarizes the implications of this view:

> The fusion of the charity ideal and the democratic credo as the ideological rationale for private initiative and control over wel-

> fare resources has made volunteerism an almost religious insti-
> tution. It obscures class divisions and contradictions and creates
> a unity which does not exist around goals which are presented
> as everybody's concern. It is an invitation to share the responsi-
> bility of the national predicaments, shifting the burden of guilt
> from men in power to the man in the street. *You* are responsi-
> ble. (p. 161)

The shifting of the burden of responsibility from the men in
power to the man in the street can be seen as a form of circumvent-
ing the more fruitful causal approaches in the analysis of social problems, that is, those that take into consideration the understanding
of the social structure. A similar, or perhaps a prototypical, cir-
cumvention of sociological thinking can be seen in the Christian
emphasis on personal guilt (and therefore responsibility) and the
possibility for individual conversion and redemption. This individ-
ualization of responsibility shifts emphasis away from the important causal factors that inhere in the socioeconomic structure or
in biology. For example, crime is seen as a personal choice and rehabilitation as a moral decision that is enhanced by individual help
and support. Socioeconomic factors in the etiology of crime and
the importance of genetic endowments in leading a productive life
are both excluded and replaced by metaphysical and moral-
interpersonal causes such as the original sin or the absence of compassion. Thus, the Christian preoccupation with the individual as
a source of both cause and remedy for social problems, and the
relegation of the origins of suffering to metaphysical and moral
realms, both tend to conspire against the acknowledgement of significant social factors. Notions that glorify individual responsibility
and individual amelioration (through conversion or therapy) are
essentially non-radical; they consider consequences, not causes. This
way of thinking, then, militates against the possibility of radical
intervention, that is, intervention that takes account of social,
economic, and genetic factors. The following statement from the
foreword of a book on volunteerism by Cull and Hardy (1974)
illustrates this individualistic approach:

> In order for progress and goodness to be realized in our society,
> we must develop greater respect for each individual and strive
> to understand in a personal way, his needs, his fears and longings
> and then relate to them. This is the essence of volunteerism. The

volunteer sees each person not as a deprived, depraved, or unfortunate object, but as a beautiful individual who has needs and aspirations—as one who requires motivation, direction, and self-esteem.

The following quotation by the head of a large volunteer organization contains most of the ideological ingredients of traditional volunteerism, which are still held, to a certain extent, by new volunteers: social atomism, moral absolutism, universal love, and commonsensical platitudes:

> Mankind is waking up to the realization that human existence is dependent upon more than materialism, the arts, government, and education . . . survival of the individual is dependent upon his unselfish interaction with other individuals and with all creation. Intrinsic to human life is the rule that the only things we really keep are those which we give away. A volunteer experiences the indisputable proof of this spiritual law. (Roupe, 1973)

Given the large numbers involved, current trends in correctional and social service volunteering can have significant implications which should not be glossed over. The rest of this chapter presents a critique of seven problematic aspects of new volunteerism pertaining to social service, correctional, and cause-oriented volunteering.

1. A Tradition of One-Dimensional Thinking

Both traditional and modern approaches of volunteerism blend well with the strictly pragmatic approaches often followed by government agencies in dealing with various social problems. The pragmatic approach in social programming considers unhealthy social conditions as problems that can be "fixed" or ameliorated through "problem-solving" efforts. Extreme forms of this approach tend to prevent people from confronting the social causes of the problem and from recognizing the philosophical and political implications of the different ways of solving the problem.

According to Marcuse (1964), defining problems and issues at the level of their concrete and situational manifestations tends to promote one-dimensional thinking, which constitutes a serious threat to freedom. Marcuse maintains that an essential requirement of freedom lies in the capacity for critical thought. Critical thinking requires a two-dimensional form of thinking, where abstract concepts, values, and theories (subjective domain) are dynamically bound to their concrete denotations (objective domain). One-dimensional thinking arises when social problems are confronted and dealt with independently of their abstract social and philosophical meanings. It also arises when abstract concepts and principles are replaced by their operationalizations (workable definitions in limited contexts), thus precluding any direct bearing on action by these concepts and principles. This disruption of the dynamic relationship between the subjective and objective domains has a dehumanizing effect on social life. It tends to pave the way for the containment and hence the domination of the individual by institutions of the social order.

One-dimensionality as a commonsensical, atomistic perspective of the social order underlies the following platitude stated from a supposedly democratic point of view. The Report of the National Advisory Council on Voluntary Action to the Government of Canada (People in Action, 1977) states:

> . . . it should be pointed out that no one institution or person bears the full responsibility for shaping life or the form of life in society. It follows that no one should be excluded from this shaping. For this reason, some form of participation is now recognized more and more as a fundamental human right in Canadian society. (p. 32)

If no one should be excluded from shaping life in a society, then all individuals and institutions with their various functions and orientations are credible, viable, and responsible. But democratic responsibility in a complex society is maintained by mandate and representation. Certain individuals are given the mandate by majority support to govern and give shape to life in a society in keeping with the principles and cultural values embodied in the institutions they control. Contemporary society is not a commune; it consists of many groups that are in conflict over economic interests, religious views, and cultural orientations, in addition to those individuals who are in conflict with the social order itself. To consider all the different and conflicting individuals and groups as viable and responsible for shaping life in a society is an absurd notion that is practically untenable. Furthermore, the pan-democratic and unconditional tolerance of the above position suggests extreme relativism—when all standards are acceptable, then no standards exist. This pseudo-democratic and tolerant perspective is analogous to the night where all cows are black. Thus the blanket of tolerance, which minimizes the need to make distinctions and take positions, achieves conflict avoidance.

The above political platitude may have more than intellectual superficiality as its basis. In making ultimate statements, individuals, paradoxically, tend to reveal some of their deep-seated drives and inclinations. In this case, one may suspect an underlying tendency towards a sociopolitical "muddle" where shapelessness and lack of social differentiation and design are, at a certain level, desired. This desire is consistent with conflict avoidance and with the previously discussed attraction of volunteers to verbal and cognitive muddles (Chapter 4). It is worth pointing out in this context an interest in the muddle at another level: the interpersonal level. The enthusiasm that social service volunteers have for personal involvement in "the community's problems" actually amounts to a variety of patterns of interpersonal interaction where the margin between work and entertainment is blurred and where the helper-helped relationship becomes confused as both parties use each other for solving personal problems. Moreover, this intimate interaction tends to create interpersonal conflicts that also require problem-solving efforts.

The anti-intellectual and concrete pragmatic approaches of volunteerism are likely to make it an ally of the containing forces of contemporary society. Whatever oppositional thrust there was in classical volunteerism is becoming less relevant to modern institutionalized volunteer settings. According to Marcuse (1964), effective opposition to the forces of domination can only come from movements that are profoundly committed to critical thought. If this is so, the movement of volunteerism that traditionally was and still is oriented towards the subordination of the intellect can hardly have a liberating impact; on the contrary, it is capable of serving the forces of social domination.

2. Volunteerism as an Agent of Pluralism

Social service volunteerism in both ideology and practice has been intimately tied both to classical liberalism and to contemporary pluralism. According to Wolf (Marcuse, Moore & Wolf, 1965), pluralism is similar to the classical liberal doctrine in that it espouses tolerance and non-interference in the private sphere. The ideology of tolerance is the state of mind that enables modern pluralistic democracy to function well. The capacity to accept competing claims as legitimate is the necessary precondition of compromise. Wolf sees the economic conception of tolerance as based on the view that human action is motivated by economic interests rather than by principles or norms. A compromise between competing interests—especially when they are quantifiable—is easier to accept than one between opposed principles. However,

> the units of society between which tolerance and mutual acceptance are to be exercised are not isolated individuals but human groups. All arguments which Mill advanced in defense of the individual's right to differ from the surrounding society are taken over in pluralistic democracy as arguments for the right of a social group to differ from other social groups. At the same time, it is assumed that the individual will belong to some group or other—which is to say, that he will identify with and internalize the values of an existing infra-national community. (p. 36)

Thus, the conservative liberalism of contemporary American politics is more than a ritual preference for the middle of any road. It is, according to Wolf, a coherent social philosophy that combines the ideas of classical liberalism with the social and cultural structures of modern capitalist society. This "hybrid doctrine" serves simultaneously a number of social functions, such as easing the conflict among antagonistic ethnic groups, diminishing the intensity of regional opposition, and integrating the whole into the hierarchical federal system. According to Wolf, the danger of this pluralism both as theory and as practice lies in its refusal to acknowledge the possibility of a "wholesale or radical reorganization of society." By portraying society as an aggregate of groups, pluralism denies the existence of the common good. By encouraging the politics of interest groups, it utilizes mechanisms that cannot lead to the discovery or the expression of the common good.

Social service volunteerism tends to endorse and promote the pluralistic conception of society as it selects as objects for its helping activity clearly demarcated sub-groups such as the physically handicapped, ex-prisoners, refugees, native groups, economically underprivileged, ethnic groups, and the like. The volunteering activity tends to influence and transform these groups in the following three ways: first, a group is rendered more conscious of itself as a result of the helping activity. Second, the group is transformed into a publicly recognized social entity. This is achieved through media exposure, particularly through the process of securing funding and "rights" for the group. Third, the created group's status is institutionalized as a distinguished social entity and becomes accepted as one of the competing groups within a pluralistic society. This is accomplished through the bureaucratic acceptance of the group and the guarantees of certain financial or other forms of tangible support.

Thus, social service volunteerism helps to integrate recipients into a group that gives them a new identity; it also tends to make the group a socially recognized entity. Such a process, which enhances the creation of self-conscious groups, can produce a level of inter-group conflict, such as the conflict between ethnic groups or the conflict between perceived deviant groups and society at large. However, the further acceptance of the group as a viable contender in the ranks of the cultural mosaic not only resolves the initial conflict, but also serves to enhance the system of pluralism itself. The system utilizes the new conflict in two ways: (a) it acts as a substitute and diversion from the more serious class conflict and (b) the credibility of the political system which assumes the role of resolving group conflicts and reintegrating groups within the overall sociopolitical structure is enhanced. The system here assumes the role of conflict reconciliation. Thus, the political system benefits both from the creation and from the reconciliation of this type of conflict.

The strategy of the Canadian federal government in encouraging immigrant ethnic groups to maintain their cultural identity through giving grants and access to media time is interesting in this context. This strategy is actually a planned adoption and promotion of pluralism as an aspect of the sociopolitical system. The similarity of this planned process to that taking place spontaneously in volunteerism is striking. The encouragement of ethnic minorities to maintain their cultural identity entails the generating of a level of inter-group conflict in society. However, this intentionally created ethnic conflict (or pseudo-conflict) tends to serve the political system functionally in the two above-mentioned ways, as a diversion from class conflict, and an enhancement of the political system itself.

3. Volunteerism: The Neutralization of Opposites

A sociopolitical problem that can be created by organized social service volunteering is its contribution to the "neutralization of opposites" process. This concept was used by Marcuse (Marcuse, Moore & Wolf, 1965) in reference to social processes in American society that tend to transform tolerance from an active to a passive state, and from practice to non-practice. Tolerance among inherently contradictory and opposed social trends within the American democratic framework tends, according to Marcuse, to neutralize opposition. The almost immediate acceptance of any new social group or trend constitutes a "repressive tolerance" which actually seeks to prevent the group from struggling to achieve power. This involves the neutralization of its conflict potential. Thus, passive tolerance serves to legitimate, compromise, and subsequently co-opt and contain the new social group within the larger social mosaic of other competing groups and trends—which amounts to social domination and repression.

According to Marcuse (Marcuse, Moore & Wolf, 1965), the catalytic mechanism that enhances the neutralization of opposites is the "objectification" process, which is highly intensified in post-industrial society. Objectification is a process through which a social entity is perceived and treated as external to and independent of human volition. This process mainly consists of the various forms of description, labelling, and analyses of social entities in styles borrowed from scientific and technical procedures. When a social movement or problematic trend is depicted objectively (quantified, described, documented, analyzed, etc.), it incurs the risk of being treated as an objective, "given," "out-there" phenomenon which, like natural phenomena, is morally and philosophically neutral. Thus, social behaviour that is controversial and to a large extent determined by human values, norms, and principles is perceived as a given objective fact that needs to be acknowledged, accepted, tolerated, and accommodated into the context of the pluralistic system. This process is enhanced by the democratic argument that nobody, neither group nor individual, is in possession of the absolute truth and capable of defining what is right and wrong, good or bad. Objectification amounts to stripping social phenomena of their subjective components, that is, their philosophical, moral, and sociopolitical significance. This involves the neutralization of their conflict or dialectical potential.

The dangers of objectification in the human and social sphere were noted by Nietzsche (1885), who suggested that when a social phenomenon is objectively depicted and analyzed, it becomes "solved" and hence it "ceases to concern us," that is, it becomes morally and philosophically neutral. For example, forms of sexual perversion can be seen as given "objective" facts in the same way that trees, rocks, and the weather are facts. It follows that these forms of behaviour should be acknowledged, studied, researched, and accommodated (accepted) within a society that espouses tolerance. This perspective ignores the fact that the behaviour in question, unlike natural phenomena, is determined, to a significant extent, by social norms that are subject to human volition and intervention. That is, the behaviour can be caused by human values (at the level of the psychosexual development of behaviour) and can also be controlled by these values through decisions and policies consistent with them. Therefore, forms of behaviour such as sexual perversion and crime cannot be treated as if they are given, "out-there" phenomena independent of moral and political choices. To treat such social phenomena as value-neutral and inevitable facts would amount to the surrender of radical political options and the maintaining of accommodation and conflict reconciliation as the only viable forms of intervention. This perspective, which undermines and neutralizes the function of moral and philosophical judgements in social analysis and intervention, tends to subordinate the human will and subsequently to deny freedom.

Among social service volunteer groups, correctional volunteering is the most problematic with respect to the above-mentioned "neutralization of opposites" process. Its cultivation of personal interaction between the law-abiding citizen and the criminal within the framework of tolerance tends to destigmatize crime and to objectify the state of being a criminal. The administrative definitions of the criminal as "inmate," "parolee," "probationer," "ex-offender," and the like contribute to the process of objectification, which tends to reduce the traditional stigma of criminality with its overall moral and social significance. The interaction of the law-abiding citizen volunteer and the offender in the cognitive context of these objectified administrative categories and in the added volunteeristic notions of "helper," "friend," "counsellor," "big brother" serves to further destigmatize and neutralize the state of the criminal.

A level of objectification of the state of the criminal can also take place through the medical model whereby crime is seen as a psychological illness and the criminal as needing treatment.[12] The process of objectification and its destigmatizing effects may have a far more negative impact on deterrence than the dramatization and romanticization of crime and the criminal through entertainment media. The moral stigma of crime may be an important factor in deterrence which society cannot afford to ignore.

A practical illustration of the neutralization of opposites in correctional volunteerism can be depicted in the following scene observed by the writer. A prisoner (convicted of heroin trafficking) was invited on a day pass as a guest speaker to a social work class by two student volunteers. During lunch, the prisoner sat with his escorting officer, his classification officer who happened to be at the university at the time, the professor, and the two student volunteers. All were talking on a first-name basis, chatting about politics and oblivious to any contradiction save, perhaps, that each had his own views on politics as well as his own way of "doing his thing."

4. Volunteerism as Covert State Domination

The doctrine of political pluralism holds that volunteer groups constitute a safeguard against the rule of the elite by distributing power over a large number of citizens' organizations. Volunteerism has often been "justified" by arguing that participation in voluntary associations assures citizens of their share in the governmental process. However, the argument fails to distinguish between participation in the decision-making process and participation in social service tasks and programs.

In contrast to the doctrine of political pluralism stands the elitist theory represented by C. Wright Mills (1956). It maintains that polit-

---

[12]The classical medical model in the understanding and treatment of health disorders centred on the paradigm of the human body as a machine composed of divisible parts. Attention, as a result, was focused on the "disease" as a medical entity and the treatment of observable bodily symptoms, while omitting the investigation of mental, emotional, and social determinants of the individual's illness. In psychology and psychiatry the medical model tended, in the same manner, to isolate mental and behaviour disorders from the context of their social relationships and identity. The medical model of mental disorder has frequently been criticized both from a behaviouristic and from a humanistic perspective. Both schools consider learning and social adaptation to be the mechanisms that produce the behaviour regarded by psychiatrists as symptoms.

ical power is not accessible to the average citizen, but, on the contrary, is held by the economic and political elites. Only in crisis situations will concessions be made to new uprising elements, groups, or views. Whereas pluralists see the revival of the frontier self-help spirit as leading to an increase in genuine democratic participation, the elitist theory would see efforts to expand volunteering as a form of "manipulation pressing citizens into unremunerated public service in order to assuage unrest of citizens' groups hardest hit by recession, unequal opportunities, and differential access to resources and political representation." (Eriksson-Joslyn, 1973-74, p. 161)

In her critique of the political implications of volunteerism, Eriksson-Joslyn (1973-74) pointed to co-optation as a mechanism that facilitates the manipulation and containment of active volunteers. Co-optation was defined by Philip Selznick (1966) as the process of absorbing new elements into the leadership or policy-determining structure of an organization as a means of averting threats to its stability or existence. Selznick distinguished two types of co-optation: formal and informal. Formal co-optation is the absorption of the dissident elements by making them share in the responsibility for power. Formal co-optation is resorted to when the legitimacy of a governing group or agency is called into question. Informal co-optation is a response to the pressure of specific centres of power within the community. The bargaining here consists of informally or tacitly giving substantial power to specific individuals or pressure groups in exchange for specific benefits or compliance.

Dunn and Langley (1976) argue the position that certain normative and structural aspects of volunteerism in criminal justice tend to constitute a form of covert domination of both client and volunteer. Behind the ideological masks of traditional bourgeois benevolence, the state is enhancing its oppressive potential through the institutionalization of the individual volunteer. They maintain that through administrative and bureaucratic control of agencies and programs, the volunteer becomes an extension of the state and this involves a form of covert domination which, in their view, is more oppressive than other forms of control delivered directly and overtly by the state. The authors do not offer an in-depth analysis of this process but advocate a "radical critique" of the liberal conception of citizen participation in order to arrive at the "demystifying of its false consciousness as benevolent, humanitarian and apolitical."

The view that the correctional volunteer can lose the dialectical position he may have in relation to the system and become an extension of it is supported by Marcuse's (1964) analysis of the one-dimensional approaches of contemporary society. Marcuse's general position on the issue of one-dimensionality is that all political systems become one-dimensional if they manage to completely displace and neutralize social critical thought. Applying the above sociopolitical conceptions to correctional volunteerism, it can be stated that the bureaucratic institutionalization of the role requirements, the selection criteria, the working methods, and the working labels of correctional volunteers will undermine the dialectical and "critical" quality of their input as independent citizens, and will render them faithful extensions of the bureaucratic organization.

A review of recent literature concerning volunteer associations in France (Mehl, 1982) reveals that a common political culture underlies the actions of a variety of recently created associations. Paradoxically, the associations, which emphasize the quality of life, represent an ostensibly non-political, but indirectly political, culture, which places them midway between state and civil society. The associations are seen as a means for expressing the class self-consciousness of the salaried and well-educated middle classes.

5. Correctional Volunteerism: Expanding the Criminal Justice Personnel

Another problem that seems to have developed with the proliferation of correctional volunteerism is that volunteers are adding new sets of roles to the already overloaded institutional superstructure built around the offender. The total number of individuals employed by federal and provincial correctional services in Canada is equivalent to one and a half times the number of prisoners incarcerated (Ministry of the Solicitor General, 1984). It can be roughly estimated that for each Canadian prisoner, five individuals are employed in agencies handling his criminal justice involvement. The functional interdependence among social institutions of contemporary society tends to exert pressure on criminal justice institutions to accommodate the services and the careers of the graduating specialists in fields such as social work, psychology, and criminology. As these professional roles increase, there is a comparative increase in the need for clients who will allow these roles to function, expertise to develop, and careers to be built. The "raw material" in criminal justice are the offenders and their personal "problems."

The self-fulfilling prophecy (Becker, 1963) is expected to operate in this system to increase rather than decrease the development of offender populations. With the convergence of charismatic "treatment-oriented" roles on offender management and rehabilitation, the operation of the self-fulfilling prophecy is expected to shift the accent from the labellings of legal and institutional authorities to those of well-paid professional staff. The first offender in particular is expected to be drawn into a role where he can receive the services and attention of a prestigious professional and where his criminal activity, his personal history, and his personal habits will come to concern the well-paid "knowledgeable" expert. This narcissistic affirmation of the offender's ego is likely to boost his offender identity, thereby accelerating his movement from primary deviance, characterized by resisting the criminal label, to secondary deviance, where the criminal label and role are accepted as parts of his self-image (cf. Becker, 1963).

New correctional volunteer programs are bringing a host of new types of professionals and successful members of the law-abiding society into contact with offenders through a variety of activities ranging from playing bridge to counselling and job finding. These contacts and relationships have become routinized as role expectations each with its own pattern and formula of social exchange (cf. Homans, 1961). As the number of volunteers increases, the number of relationships and role expectations will also increase. As a result, the offender may be mobilized (through the operation of the self-fulfilling process) to embrace and maintain his role as an offender in order to fulfill these mushrooming role expectations which can be "narcissistically" flattering and existentially meaningful to him.

Intelligent prisoners are becoming aware of the vast system of roles and professions that have become symbiotically contingent upon their role as criminals.[13] One inmate apparently had his self-

---

[13]During the mid- and late seventies the writer worked as a clinical criminologist with a psychiatric centre for the Penitentiary Services, operated from a Federal Prison for Women. At any time during that period it was possible to identify at least half a dozen programs carried on by volunteers from the local university. Programs such as dance therapy, drama and acting, transactional analysis, transcendental meditation, women's rights, and public speaking were added to the

esteem flattered by this realization, for he wrote to me saying, "Not only do we provide employment for unskilled guards, we also help psychologists, psychiatrists, social workers, criminologists, chaplains, and Salvation Army Corps stay in business . . . we are now being called upon to keep volunteer groups occupied."

6. Pseudo-Conflict as Neutralization of Conflict

It is in the context of cause-oriented volunteerism that the theatrical component of conflict resolution assumes its most dangerous form. For example, when a socially important issue arises, such as in the case of environmental pollution, these volunteers are readily mobilized. Their action is almost always a self-exhibition demonstration where their colourful selves, placards, and signs are displayed and accompanied by chants and noise. Their major goal is to attract media attention. After receiving media coverage, and a token official response, they disperse with the feeling of "mission accomplished." Though noisy, they are usually peaceful, and confrontation with police or other assertive behaviour is infrequent or accidental.

The socially destructive aspects of this approach consist in the following:

(a)   it takes the initiative away from more radical elements in the population who may be slower to react but who may be prepared, once they react, to utilize more effective approaches;

(b)   its passive exhibitionistic display of the issue allows authorities to comply in the same verbal manner, to take their time, and to turn the problem over to bureaucratic and legal agencies where action is delayed and compromised;

(c)   its appeal to media coverage and the capturing of public attention tends to become a goal in itself which constitutes a substitute for more organized or confrontative forms of action;

(d)   the street exhibition of the problem and the subsequent media presentation of it may not serve to engender action to con-

---

institution-sponsored ones such as upgrading of education, fine arts, and social skills courses. Intelligent inmates who would have benefited from prolonged counselling in psychotherapy became so involved with all this influx of activities that the two institution psychologists had a difficult time enlisting clients. Eventually the junior psychologist asked for transference in quest of more intensive "experience," which is a necessary ingredient of expertise.

front the problem but, by creating the impression that it has been "attended to," actually may serve to foster complacency and inaction. It can also create a process similar to mourning. Mourning is a mental and emotional preoccupation with a lost object that serves ultimately to achieve the individual's reconciliation with the fact of loss or death of the object. In the same manner, the repetitious presentations of cases of environment pollution, for example, can produce a mourning effect, reconciling the public to the fact that the devastation of the environment is an inevitable fact. Thus, instead of mobilizing people, excessive public exposure can have the opposite effect: bringing about reconciliation and acceptance. It appears that confrontative action, which may have active aggression as its biopsychological prototype, is most capable of maintaining people's motivation for effective action.

If confrontative measures such as damaging the industry responsible for pollution, or assaulting the responsible directors, were used instead of exhibitionistic ones, the response from bureaucracy would be quicker and more efficient. Such confrontative measures can deter potential polluters more effectively than legal sanctions. Passive exhibitionistic protests fail to exert direct pressure either on government agencies or on the culprit companies themselves.

A good example of the low level of effectiveness of this passive media-oriented approach can be seen in the acid rain pollution problem. After eight years of proving and exposing the fact that sulfur dioxide emission from coal-burning industries in the United States and Canada is killing wild life, especially the populations of Canadian lakes through acid rain, hardly any measures to control emissions have been made by the industries or imposed by political administrations. In 1986 political pressure by the Canadian government succeeded in making the American administration acknowledge the existence of the problem, after a period of delay justified by the supposed need to allocate funds for researching acid rain. Such delays in responding to serious ecological threats is symptomatic of the inadequacy of the political pressure exerted by the environmentalists. Another example of the inadequacy of the passive exhibitionistic approach of cause-oriented volunteers can be seen in the case of the nuclear plant at Diablo Canyon, California. The environmental protest groups waited until the plant was almost completed in 1981 before they were mobilized to protest in their picnic formations, with their children, pets, and lunch baskets. Compare this approach with the confrontative and persistent attempts of Japanese groups to block the expansion of Tokyo's Narita airport, or to the courageous attempts by Greenpeace ships to disrupt whaling operations (sometimes by ramming the whaling ship), which helped bring to a halt the uncontrolled killing of whales.

It must be noted that media coverage and publicity are vital components of the success of a social cause, but publicity by itself cannot make a cause. Furthermore, if publicity is bestowed lavishly in support of a widely supported cause, it can weaken that cause. The environmental issue is the central social and human cause that, in the opinion of this writer, is hurt most by cause-oriented volunteers. The ritualization of action into exhibitionistic protests (e.g., media coverage of someone climbing a smelter's chimney to protest acid rain), the romanticization and lamentations (mourning) of the ecological victim, and the striving to "inform the public" with information about the details of pollution—all serve to dissipate stamina, long-term planning, and effective political action in the defence of the environment. Through the lack of effective action by these volunteers, environmental consciousness becomes a ritual, a passive consciousness or tolerance that mourns rather than challenges the gradual devastation of the natural ecology.

The narcissistic interest in theatrical self-display tends to betray the stated purpose of cause-oriented volunteerism. It drastically compromises the intention to be effective in promoting the position taken. An example:

> About 100 women and men demonstrated against a Montreal porn theatre February 13, after its gala opening promised clients the hardest core pornography available in the city. Shouting "our bodies are not for sale", the demonstrators marched in front of the Cinema X urging passersby to boycott the theatre . . . the director of the theatre defended himself, stating that his shows would not contain violence. (*Fulcrum*, February 25, 1982, University of Ottawa)

It should be mentioned in this context that high and continuous media exposure can have a positive effect on certain issues. The progress made in civil rights in the last twenty years is, no doubt, an example. But not all issues can be enhanced by media exposure and conditioning. The problem of street crime, like that of ecology, can be negatively affected by the passive consciousness involved in intensive media exposure: news coverage, discussion, and presentation in the context of entertainment. Such preoccupation with an issue activates processes of objectification and value-neutralization which foster the development of a level of tacit reconciliation with anti-social behaviour. The repeated presentation of street crime in the news and entertainment media appears to have succeeded in reconciling citizens to the "fact" of street crime despite the curtailment it entails of the citizens' freedom to walk the city streets at night, and despite the blemish this curtailment inflicts on the image of a society that champions all kinds of freedom.

7. Psychological Parasitism as Conflict Avoidance

Close observation of volunteer-offender interaction can reveal, among many other relationships, a particularly interesting and subtle relationship that can have significant social implications. Violent offenders who are reasonably intelligent and socially skilled (e.g., many bank robbers) tend to attract volunteers who have an inability for direct aggression. The declared motives of these volunteers for their particular interest in violent offenders revolve around "problem-solving" notions or assume (among those educated in the social sciences) a "research" interest in violence. From a psychoanalytic perspective, the attraction of this type of volunteer to the violent offender can be interpreted as motivated by the opportunity afforded for vicarious expression of the volunteer's own unsuccessfully expressed aggressivity. It may be that the volunteer also has a "problem" with aggression: his drive may be weakened or repressed to the extent that he cannot actively express it, or he lacks the psychic capacity to cope with its expression. The association with the violent offender affords such a volunteer a vicarious and safe mode of getting in touch with his own aggression: an expression by identification, without having to pay the offender's price for it.

Under more normal and healthier conditions, people tend to affirm, directly or indirectly, the behaviour they vicariously enjoy. The cheering of spectators at a bull fight affirms that violent sport and ensures its continuity. An example of a less direct affirmation of physical violence is the case of fights and brawls that take place during sport games such as hockey. These fights are not officially endorsed; nevertheless, their vicarious enjoyment by the audience—expressed in cheering—tends to affirm this type of violent expression; officials tend to tolerate it and athletes engage in it partly for the purpose of entertaining and thrilling the spectators. An example of a more common form of vicarious participation in aggressive expression is the case of a noted professor and scholar who took to the habit of joining a group of construction workers in drinks in a tavern frequented by blue-collar workers. He enjoyed their spontaneous expression of aggression in brawls and other forms of "physical humour," a mode of self-expression that for him was drastically curtailed by his academic life. He did not participate in their mode of expression but he did not interfere with it, nor did he try to convert them to his cerebral and verbal style. As a result they liked him, felt at ease with him, and even indulged more in their ways in order to please him.

In the case of the correctional volunteer, the role setting and the ideology that defines violent behaviour as a "problem" or "sickness" discourage any due affirmation of the overt aggressive mode (e.g., the viability of overt aggression as healthier than the totally self-destructive one). The volunteer, as a result, is encouraged to repress or deny any vicarious interest in violent aggression, which can result in the deployment of the reaction-formation mechanism. Being a defence against the aggression drive, this reaction-formation tends to promote an absolutist attitude towards violent aggression as bad in itself, and accordingly, preclude any positive and socially balanced evaluation of the offender's mode of criminal assertion.

Therefore, instead of a minimal positive affirmation of the behaviour vicariously enjoyed, there is a total depreciation and denial of it, a reaction that prevents an exchange relationship and fosters a parasitic one. Parasitism is typically an association where the parasite feeds on the desired element in the host until the host is either depleted of that resource, or rendered unbalanced (ill) or eventually incapable of sustaining the resource (dead). In the symbiotic relationship two organisms engage in mutual exchange of needed elements or services without damaging each other; however, the parasite is insensitive to the needs of the host and tends to damage it. Thus, the volunteer behaves in a parasitic fashion towards the violent offender: he vicariously enjoys the offender's aggressiveness (feeds on it) and at the same time seeks to denounce, discourage, and eradicate it through approaches inspired by absolutely held moral attitudes and the medical model. The result (at least in theory) is that the offender's personality is altered in such a way that he can no longer produce the behaviour that attracted the volunteer in the first place.

The volunteer's relationship with the violent offender can be seen as representing a progression from conflict reconciliation to conflict avoidance. The volunteer is attracted to the conflict in the context of reducing and controlling the offender's violent behaviour. With the operation of the above-mentioned parasitic process, the initial reconciliation approach progresses towards the dissipation and denial of violent aggression—a relationship consistent with conflict avoidance. But not all conflict is dysfunctional to the extent that it should be resolved at any time and by any means available. At the social level, conflict can have many positive functions (see Coser, 1956). At the interpersonal level conflict involving violence can also have its functional aspects within the given social order. This has been dramatized in the highly successful 1971 film of Stanley Kubrick, "Clockwork Orange," which shows how the total curbing of violent aggression in an individual can be as problematic as the violence itself.

A healthier approach to the assessment of the violent offender's socially dysfunctional behaviour would be to evaluate this behaviour at two levels: first, at the level of its specific context where the degree of legal responsibility and the extent of damage or injury incurred are examined; second, at the level of the larger social context where the symbolic and social significance of the violent behaviour is examined. The following questions may be considered at the second level: was the violent behaviour expressed as a response to other generalized and less obvious forms of social oppression? Does the violent behaviour contain any ethical or other socially redeeming qualities such as courage, defence of dignity, or the affirmation of an aspect of justice in the broad and social sense? What is the deterrent impact of the violent behaviour on forms of nonviolent aggression? When these two levels of behaviour are considered, a dialectical process is generated between them which paves the way for a balanced and just perception of the problem behaviour. This perspective automatically discourages narrow, one-dimensional, and absolutist perceptions based on moral values or on concrete applications of the medical model.

An objective analysis of violent behaviour reveals that violent aggression is only one aspect of aggression, much of which (in contemporary society) is non-violent, passive, and impersonal. Violent aggression can often be a response to other forms of non-violent aggression, damage, and oppression. Furthermore, violent aggression may serve an important function in balancing and deterring passive forms of aggression such as deceit, legal artifice, cunning, and manipulation, which tend to multiply in social settings where the threat of violent reaction has been virtually eliminated (see Sorel, 1907). Given the present social order, which involves intricate and subtle forms of oppression and damage, any absolutist negative attitude towards violent aggression is not only hypocritical, but may be socially harmful.

An example of the psychological parasitism described above can be seen in the following case. The writer had the opportunity to observe the progress of an intelligent and handsome youthful offender after he was transferred from a maximum to a medium security penitentiary. He had been involved in a series of crimes involving violence, including a few well-executed armed robberies. During his incarceration at the maximum security penitentiary, he became involved in prison politics and in the promotion of prisoners' rights, and tended to dominate the inmate committee. He was well-spoken, articulate, and well-read. His transfer appeared to have been an attempt to get rid of him and his politicizing of prisoners in the maximum security institution. Soon after his arrival at the medium security penitentiary, he was courted by half a dozen middle-class professional volunteers. The most active among them were two professors from the department of theology at the local university, and a girl majoring in psychology who subsequently became his fiancée while he was still in prison. There were books, visits, educational counselling, philosophical and theological discussions, spiritual reunions, and there were day passes for lunches with his volunteers, their families, and their academic friends. His original intention had been to study political sciences by correspondence and to enter politics after release. However, he was counselled to shift to psychology and religion and he received all academic assistance in that direction from his volunteer "friends." After two years of "differential association" with his prestigious and highly dedicated group of academics, he began to evidence changes in his attitude and views. He endorsed pacifist and individualistic views which were a drastic departure from the original radical and socially conscious positions which he used to discuss at length with this writer. When I confronted him with the fact of this change and that it did not, philosophically speaking, appear to be for the better, he totally avoided me. His transformation did not seem to be manipulative play-acting for it would not have contributed to an early release; he was scheduled for parole in due legal time regardless of his behaviour. The psychiatric evaluations of him indicated that he was not a psychopathic personality. The change that he evidenced seemed to be genuine; his fiancée, whom he was seriously preparing to marry, was an ardent pacifist.

In this writer's opinion such is a high price for rehabilitation and "settling down." This man would have been capable of giving more to society if he had become involved in a serious political movement. Given the banal and flaccid personalities that predominate in the political scene in Canada, individuals with his charismatic style, idealism, and active thrust (he diverted his thrust towards individualistic and consumeristic pursuits) could contribute positively to the quality of political behaviour.

In summary, I have argued that a volunteer suffering from repressions and inadequacies at the level of his aggressive and oppositional drives may be vicariously attracted to an offender who is at ease in this mode of personal and social expression. Due to the impact of moral notions and the role structure of the volunteer, and due to the reaction-formation that ensues, the volunteer becomes psychologically mobilized to "solve" and dissipate not only the offender's problem behaviour (violent expression in service of egoistic and anti-social goals) but also his confrontative style. The volunteer usually has at his disposal privileges, prestige, intellectual and social skills with which he can engender change in the offender's style. The relationship is essentially parasitic at the psychological level and tends to progress from a conflict reconciliation type of relationship to that of conflict avoidance. In this book conflict avoidance is considered to be psychologically and socially unhealthy. If this parasitic psychological relationship takes place in a large number of cases and in similar social settings, then it becomes a socially significant process in which conflicts that need to be addressed are only neutralized and avoided.

Chapter 6

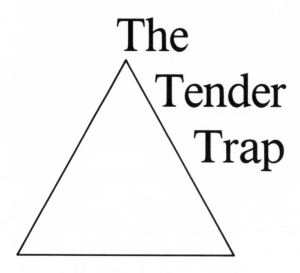

The
Tender
Trap

In this final chapter I wish to consider some additional implications of my research and speculation about those individuals who have an affinity for conflict avoidance. Specifically, I wish to discuss an enigma they present: while appearing through their reduction of interpersonal and social conflict to make a major and positive contribution to society, they may actually represent a force capable of significant social destructiveness.

Conflict Avoidance and Passive-Aggression

In order to clarify my reasoning, it is first necessary to discuss a concept that has long been recognized in the context of individual adjustment but has seldom been considered in terms of its social implications: passive-aggression. It has often been noted that there are two basic and qualitatively different modes of aggressive behaviour: active and passive. Active aggression is that form of aggression in which both the act and the target are tangible and manifest. Most forms of violent aggression belong to the active mode: the individual acts violently towards an object or individual that is the target of the perpetrator's aggressive motivation. Passive-aggression, however, is less easily recognized. It is aggression that does not *appear* to be aggression. It is indirect, covert, or masked—aggression that is expressed in a passive form.

All forms of aggression can be classified as belonging to either an active or a passive mode. This classification can be applied to all levels of behaviour: physical, emotional, cognitive, and verbal. To equate violence, which is a mode of aggression, with the generic concept of aggression would be utterly misleading. In contemporary post-industrial society, aggression is most often expressed through passive-aggressive modes, although violent aggression receives the greater part of public attention and interest.

The predominance of the passive mode of aggression in contemporary society is largely dictated by the highly complex organizations that control most aspects of an individual's life. Complex organizations facilitate the expression of passive-aggression in two ways: first, many individuals use the formal structures of an organization as weapons for "aggressing" passively against others. For example, an otherwise non-assertive employee can readily manage to become distressingly aggressive through the use of deliberate delaying procedures in routine matters, or by excessive rule-following behaviour, or by mischievous dissemination of information. Wilfully and knowingly or not, such individuals can be highly aggressive while behaving in ways that for all intents and purposes are perfectly legitimate and proper. Moreover, they can be "sweet," charming, self-effacing, and abundantly apologetic while so doing. Second, individuals can utilize an organizational structure and its rules to camouflage themselves from their victims, who are often unable to identify the source of aggression and, therefore, unable to retaliate against this source. It is worth mentioning in this context that forms of camouflage behaviour in both predation and defence exist in most living species: insects, marine animals, birds, and mammals. The recent growth in the size and complexity of the formal organization is actually opening new avenues for the expression of passive-aggression that utilizes camouflage strategies. Thus, a compatibility and mutual reinforcement may now exist between phylogenetically archaic behavioural forms and socially highly advanced settings. This relationship can be best appreciated and studied from an ethological perspective.

The absence of overt conflict in a society need not imply a state of social health and peace. Similarly, individuals who avoid conflict and recoil from engaging in direct and fully conscious confrontations are not necessarily healthy or psychologically at peace, nor are they necessarily innocent of behaviour that is damaging to society. Psychopathologists have long recognized that passive-aggression is often at the root of the etiology of depression, various psychosomatic illnesses, and personal or social ineffectiveness (Parsons & Wicks, 1983).

Sociologically speaking, the passive-aggressive personality uses his or her social or occupational role as a means of expressing aggressive needs which the individual cannot or will not express directly. By using, or misusing, one's role in this manner, one damages the status of the role. By sabotaging the operation of social roles (e.g., parent, public official) in such a way, passive-aggressive individuals can render a great deal of damage at all levels of social life. "You have not seen much of life if you have not seen the hand that kills tenderly," says Nietzsche.

Reducing the level of aggression in a society cannot be achieved by attempting to eliminate or suppress all violence or all avenues of direct aggression. On the contrary, the more society suppresses direct aggression, the more rampant will passive-aggression be. As suggested earlier in this book, active aggression and passive-aggression can balance and contain each other. For example, violent aggression can be controlled by means of threats that utilize legal or formally structured procedures. Conversely, the threat of violence can deter and curb passive-aggression expressed at both the interpersonal and organizational levels. Evidence gathered by the author from prisons and other institutional settings suggests that individuals with a passive-aggressive personality disorder tend to be most effectively contained by threats that are direct and explicit in nature, particularly those that are violent. Attempts to counteract the antisocial behaviour of these personalities by covert and bureaucratic manipulation will often serve to stimulate their passive-aggressive behaviour.[14]

The research and analysis described in Chapters 3 and 4 presented a profile of an individual who feels uneasy with direct con-

---

[14]Although certain forms of violent expression can be learned, lowering the level of aggression in a society is achieved by reducing the conditions that produce and perpetuate aggression, such as inequality, structured competition, political corruption, overcrowdedness and environmental stressors, unemployment, relative deprivation, and anomie.

frontation, who tends to respond to serious social issues either by compromise and appeasement, or by neutralization and avoidance of conflict. The social orientation of this type of individual is in harmony with currently expanding institutional and cultural controls that are conducive to passive-aggression. The conflict-reducing orientation and style of these individuals help in tilting the balance of aggression in favour of the passive-aggressive mode. When normative and structural controls restrict access to modes of direct aggression, the balancing and deterrent impact of active on passive aggression is curtailed. Such restrictions lead to the increase of cunning, deceit, legal artifice, and many other forms of institutional manipulation that augment psychological oppression and increase stress diseases and self-destructive behaviour in a society.

Conflict Avoidance and the Sociopolitical System

There is, of course, a strong sociopolitical force that contributes to an unhealthy disturbance of balance between the two modes of aggression. It is the vested interest of the "power elite" to render as unacceptable or unfashionable, and to otherwise eliminate, all forms of organized violence as political means. Governments in the West have been able over time to institutionalize, displace, appease, and manage class conflict through non-violent means such as the separation of ownership from management in industries and the settlement of wage disputes through contract negotiations (Dahrendorf, 1959). However, political violence remains the most dreaded threat to the stability and the continuity of the system. This is because of the disruptive and unpredictable consequences of violence.

The major beneficiary in a society that has a large number of individuals who are motivated towards conflict reconciliation and conflict avoidance is the sociopolitical establishment. However, it is not the case that the establishment merely remains passive and benefits from the behaviour of such people; it actively encourages and promotes such behaviour. For example, the trend of lifting moral sanctions from a great many sexual behaviours and the proliferation of the "sexual revolution" tend to resolve conflict in favour of the capitalist system. The pursuit of varied sexual contacts serves to direct energy away from the political sphere. Sexual hedonism promotes a form of self-indulgence that engages and dissipates psychic energy within purely individualistic avenues and for a lengthy period of a person's life.

According to the Freudian theory, the sexual drive is not biologically structured at birth; it acquires its goals and orientations in the course of the psychosexual development of the individual. For the past ninety years, clinical data have confirmed this claim through accounts of a large number of sexual idiosyncrasies and perversions exhibited by different individuals. Each individual has a variety of actual and latent forms of sexual preferences. When the expression of a certain form of sexual behaviour is blocked by social constraints, fantasy tends to express and at the same time restrain the particular drive. Under permissive sociocultural conditions, the sexual menu of an individual expands, as do the sexual pursuits that draw upon his time and energy. Having an extra-marital affair or multiple sex partners represents not only new opportunities for fun, but also alternate avenues for the expenditure of time and energy, since intimate relationships tend to be complex and demanding. Furthermore, as one sexual appetite is satisfied, new ones tend to surface. By the time an individual explores and satisfies his private opportunities and tastes, and by the time he arrives at the phase of sexual "wisdom," twenty of his most vital years may have elapsed. This libidinal energy and time invested in individualistic pursuits and the ensuing interpersonal conflicts diminish the energy that can be utilized in collectively oriented endeavours that involve political thinking and action. Moreover, the privatization of an individual's social endeavours promotes self-centredness and narcissism (Lasch, 1979).

The notion popular in the sixties that sexual liberation will lead to political liberation proved to be a misconceived, erroneous notion, for the opposite appears to have taken place. The liberationists of that period failed to appreciate Freud's (1928) position, presented in his *Civilization and Its Discontents*, that sexual repression is part of the total and inevitable social repression dictated by civilization. The more complex society becomes, the greater is the degree of repression of the instincts. Surplus restriction may be placed on sex at certain periods, but the fact that sexual repression is an inevitable demand of civilization was never doubted by Freud. The liberationists of the sixties thought that the tail could wag the dog and failed to comprehend the tenacity and adaptability of the sociopolitical system in that it could take their tools of liberation and use them to its advantage. Thus, the sexual revolution was eventually adopted by those at the top. For instance, the legalization of homosexuality was brought forward through legislation by parliaments and other legislative bodies after periods of debate, rather than due to popular pressure. Had there been a referendum on the issue, it is very likely that the laws would not have been passed. The religious and moral bodies exerted only token or no resistance and some of them were prepared to go along with the trend and accommodate the "sinful" behaviour. "Big Brother" has been tacitly recommending "go and enjoy yourself" as a prescription against the pursuit of political mischief. The only significant "counter revolutionary" force appears to have come from AIDS, a drastic biological threat which has been slowing down the sexual revolution.

It can also be observed that the sociopolitical establishment has been encouraging the feminist movement and accommodating to it in the context of conflict neutralization. The movement can lend itself functionally to the system in two ways.

First, the feminist ideology has been creating a biological dialectic or a pseudo-conflict between the sexes which can act as a displacement substitute for class conflict. The grievances and the "war" of women against men, constantly presented through the media, tend to centre on the following six themes: (1) Rebellion theme: women are expected to rebel against the domination perceived to be imposed by men, and against discrimination in favour of men. (2) Blameworthiness theme: men have been responsible for the plight of women in the past. The individualized version of this theme blames the individual failures of women on men. (3) Violence theme: men are potential rapists. (4) Competition theme: men are challenged as biological entities; an example is the controversy over girls joining boys' hockey and football teams. (5) Progress theme: battles for equal rights are being won, and gains are being consolidated—thanks to the fairness and conflict reconciliation efforts of politicians who champion the cause of progress. (6) Triumph theme: with battles won there is the anticipation of final triumph in the achievement of complete equality. However, for some feminists triumph does not stop at achieving complete equality with men. Beneath the veneer of equal rights lurks the ultimate goal of the triumph of feminism itself, where the "oppressed" finally overcome and establish their own "just rule," a female-dominated society. The excessive preoccupation with and promotion of the ideology that pits the sexes against each other can generate socially regressive and disintegrative conflicts between men and women at the interpersonal level and within the family organization.

The second functional advantage for the sociopolitical system lies in the negative orientation of the feminist movement towards the use of violent aggression in political matters. Many feminists perceive violence as a symbol of male domination and denounce it as uncivilized and pathological. Violent aggression appears to be an enemy shared by the economic elite and the feminist movement in its present psychosocial and political expression. Some social analysts argue that the feminist movement has not only been tolerated by the power elite, but has also been tacitly supported by those in power through the facilitation of the entry of women into key administrative and political positions. The ranks of the armed forces are now being opened to women despite the lack of popular demand by women for such roles. Women seem to hold the promise of being more comfortable at the bargaining table, more verbal than violent in demonstrations, more psychologically inclined towards the indirect expression of aggression, and thus more adaptive to the modes of control demanded by complex organizations. Consequently, women can be perceived as a potentially less disruptive, destabilizing force than men.

It should be noted in this context that any trend that promotes the weakening and disintegration of cohesive collectivities such as the family and organized political groups tends to serve the interests of the present capitalist system. Cohesive social groups demand a binding commitment on various levels of individual behaviour. They are the breeding grounds for integrated ideological thinking, and they are capable of generating serious and destabilizing political conflicts. The system is better protected by the preponderance of loose collectivities such as sports teams, clubs, and fraternities that engage individuals partially or superficially. These loose collectivities are incapable of generating significant political conflict; they can create only limited or pseudo-conflict. Once cohesive social groups no longer constitute the basic units of a society and are replaced by loose collectivities, the population is reduced to a herd of individual consumers that can be totally manipulated by the system.

"Big Brother" may not always be explicitly conscious of what he does; however, his behaviour remains purposeful and intentional.

A social group that wields a large segment of the socioeconomic power is also equipped with a collective unconscious intelligence (Fromm, 1962) that tends to convert efforts to its advantage. A socioeconomic power elite may not be responsible for creating social movements or trends in a complex society, but it is certain that it will attempt to manipulate, disseminate, or catalyze a social trend in directions compatible with its advantage. This can be carried out spontaneously and unconsciously without the articulation of any explicit plan. Given the vast amount of knowledge in the behavioural and biological sciences, and given the powerful techniques of electronic communication, an alarming prospect arises: in its quest for making profits, the capitalist establishment will overlook no trick or technique in manipulating, transforming, experimenting with, and consequently deforming, human nature as we know it. For example, the ongoing and systematic process of shifting moral taboos (shameful, sinful, immoral) from deviant forms of sex onto violence is bound to have serious social consequences.[15] Direct forms of aggression, as a result, become alienated from meaningful social and political action and forced into desperate or pathological forms of expression such as bizarre mass murder, suicide, and addiction.[16] Furthermore, the sexualization of hitherto sex-inhibited areas of social interaction (in relating to children, friendships, politics, etc.) tends to invite socially disintegrative conflicts

---

[15]Recent campaigners for the control of pornography, when pressed to justify their demands, often claimed that pornography can lead to violence. The old-time reasons that pornography invites debauchery, hedonism, sin, immorality, etc., seem to have been suddenly forgotten. It is interesting to observe how "violence" is gradually being made to replace "vice."

[16]An illustration of such alienated and pathological expressions of aggression can be seen in recent incidents: in several cases an individual randomly fired at people walking in the street, and in another case someone in New York smuggled into a drugstore Tylenol capsules laced with cyanide, which resulted in the death of eight people who happened to buy the poisoned bottles. The first type of incident represents a form of active aggression, the second a passive-aggressive form. The two incidents, however, are similar in that they employ aggression in an "ego-alien" manner, where the aggressive activity is dissociated from the person's self, which includes faculties for the evaluation and selection of action. Sociologically speaking, the aggressive activity is expressed in an anomic context independent of any normative structuring, indicating that the perpetrator is suffering from severe anomia. Thus, aggression which can be a meaningful and instrumental behaviour becomes an alien and meaningless tension that needs to be reduced like tension in a full bladder.

into central social relationships. An unrestrained Eros can be as deadly as Thanatos: a message deduced from the Freudian theory by Marcuse (1956) in his book *Eros and Civilization.*

The Conflict Resolution Syndrome and Current Social Problems

Where does an individual characterized by the Conflict Resolution Syndrome (or the conflict avoidance type of individual) stand with respect to the above social trends and processes? Given his tolerant and non-oppositional orientation at all major levels of functioning, he stands as a catalyst or a compliant victim to these socially disintegrating trends. For example, when such individuals take a position against current trends of sexual permissiveness and hedonism, they typically do so through adherence to a metaphysically bound religious belief reinforced by a church or group of co-believers. But unlike the traditional religious fundamentalists who aggressively sought to eliminate sin, contemporary groups composed of this type are highly tolerant of sin and tend to peacefully coexist with it. They attempt to overcome not by confrontative challenge but by conversion of others to their faith, so that the weight of numbers becomes the decisive factor. However, this tolerance appears to be born out of psychic impotence rather than from a strong attachment to democratic ideals. Such "passive" tolerance tends to rob society of the benefits of an "active" conditional tolerance that dialectically restrains a social trend from taking on extreme pathological dimensions.

The most dangerous threat that individuals characterized by the Conflict Resolution Syndrome pose to Western society, and consequently to the future of humanity, lies in their persistent attempts to address all major social and global problems, and in so doing to offer solutions that are basically adapted to their own psychological needs and capacities rather than solutions dictated by the objective conditions of the problem addressed. They address and seek to deal with such major social and global problems as Third World poverty and starvation, overpopulation, destruction and pollution of the ecology, threat of nuclear war, crime, addiction, family disorganization, and the like. But their approach to these problems typically distorts and compromises any adequate solutions in three major ways. First, they construe the problem in an extremely concrete and therefore limited way, thereby failing to recognize or consider broader social and long-term solutions or the consequences of their problem-solving actions. Second, they utilize exhibitionistic media-oriented approaches that are geared to superficial and compromised solutions. Third, they appeal to spiritual and moral absolutes rather than to a social theory or a realistic and integrated vision of reality.

The following are some examples of the short-term compromised and inadequate solutions advocated or carried out by these types of individuals. Poverty and starvation in the Third World are defined concretely and presented as problems that can be solved by relief programs involving the soliciting of donations by the appeal to notions of sympathy and humanitarian concern. Frequently there is a total lack of interest in and response to the underlying causes of these "problems"; their humanitarian-appearing actions at best provide only temporary relief and create false hopes and expectancies that the woes can be eliminated by these methods. At worst, they serve to divert attention from the underlying causes and, in so doing, may vindicate them. They communicate a message: the problem is the symptom, not the disease. Similarly, escalating crime rates, alcoholism, and drug addiction are reacted to by a vast array of rehabilitation and treatment programs that serve to displace interest in tackling the significant underlying socioeconomic causes and absorb the energies that might otherwise be directed to remedying such conditions. Defence of the environment is sought through exhibitionistic campaigns that stop at public awareness and media lamentations of the danger to the ecology. Such vain outcries avoid confrontation with those who are responsible for the pollution.

These approaches are not only weak and ineffective; they also serve to distort the perception of the problem itself. The problem is operationally defined in terms of the selected intervention strategy. For example, poverty and starvation in Third World countries come to be perceived as a humanitarian challenge requiring relief feeding, improved aid programs, and the enlistment of enthusiastic humanitarians. The recent enlistment of rock stars in fund raising for the hungry is a further step in the universalizing and ritualizing of these trivial measures. While the sponsors of these campaigns are enthusiastically preoccupied with fund raising and relief work, crucial causal factors such as over-population are often dismissed or confronted superficially.

I suggest that the deep-seated personality needs tend to force themselves on the perception of the social problem and on the methods of intervention selected and supported. The line of action followed becomes a compromise, or rather a psychosocial adjustment, between the personality needs of conflict resolution and the demands of the relevant objective conditions. The distortion of perspective and the inadequate means of confronting the problem combine to perpetuate the tremendous social cost of this adjustment.

The tenacity by which such types of individuals hold on to particular modes of problem-solving and interaction can be observed among ardent "do-gooders" and missionaries. Among these individuals, sympathy, pity, and the activity of charitable work often become ends in themselves. Their insistence on dealing with poverty and other human suffering through charitable and altruistic intervention makes one wonder about the existence of an unconscious affirmation of human misery, since its presence affords them the task of ameliorating it. Radical social solutions to poverty and to other forms of social victimization were seldom appealing to missionaries because such solutions are not only confrontative but also tend to eliminate the teleological concerns revolving around charity. I would argue that a persistent allegiance to a mode of intervention that inadequately meets its espoused goal indicates a primary allegiance to personal needs met through that mode, and that these needs are satisfied not only at the expense of the reality and ultimate solution of the problem, but at the expense of the victims of that problem.

There is, in my view, something fundamentally self-serving, egocentric, and possibly narcissistic in the behaviour of such individuals, even though their actions are couched in socially palatable expressions of humanitarianism. The egocentric thinking of many such religiously devout individuals is reflected in the tenacity with which they hold to their "truth" and their "humanitarian" methods against critical reasoning. I suggest that behind many forms of malignant aggression against society lurks some sort of camouflaged egocentric or narcissistic force.

It is through a complex interaction with sociological factors that such narcissistically bound psychological variables engender significant social and political consequences. In the case of social service volunteerism the process appears to take place in the following way: certain individuals seek out certain volunteer roles that are in harmony with some of their personal needs and particularly their conflict resolution needs. This state of harmony fosters long-term adaptation to the role and in turn enables their personal needs (expressed in terms of their practical approaches and ideas) to influence and mould the role structure to their favour, thus establishing the social character of the role. Under the impact of social change, social structure variables such as the increase of leisure time, cuts in social service spending, or support by the political system may operate to enhance these roles. This often leads to increased recruitment of volunteers and the expansion and proliferation of volunteer agencies. Individuals characterized by the Conflict Resolution Syndrome are therefore able to consolidate their power (through selectively recruiting their own kind) and can come to dominate large social organizations. From a position of numerical and bureaucratic dominance such individuals can influence the social, political, and cultural order of society.

Individuals characterized by the Conflict Resolution Syndrome can, under favourable conditions, be highly successful in the acquisition of political power. The present demands for political candidacy are well suited to this conflict avoidance personality type. The basic demands for public office are public speaking and other theatrical skills involved in saying and doing what appeals to the voters. The presentation of pragmatic schemes, solutions, and promises requires no great intellectual skills. Except for the declarations of general ideological slogans, the political process does not call upon the intellectual ability to conceptualize and integrate the philosophic, economic, and sociopolitical variables involved in a political office in time and place. The problem arises when this individual achieves an authoritative political office. He is likely to be traumatized by the power vested in the office and may not know what to do with it. The easy rider on ballots has his lame leg riding with him; he will feel it most markedly when he assumes office. In periods of crisis or in unusual historical conditions where crucial decisions have to be made, the conflict avoidant type may prove to be a disaster.

Many examples can be drawn from history where, in a situation of crisis, this type of individual proved to be not only ineffectual but destructive. For example, the personality of Woodrow Wilson, as described by William Bullit and Sigmund Freud (1920), is strikingly similar to my description of the conflict avoidant type. During the Treaty of Versailles negotiations he consistently failed to exert sufficient pressure on Britain and France to temper their punitive conditions on Germany, conditions that paved the way for the Second World War. The United States had emerged after the First World War as the most powerful economic world force, while France and Britain were in a state of economic exhaustion. Wilson had only to wield economic pressures against Britain and France to force a more reasonable treaty with Germany, but he lacked the personal force to assert his wishes or to confront them. He was extremely impressive when it came to oratory and the advocation of political or spiritual ideals. The personality weakness and flaccidity of an incumbent Wilson, in times of crisis, can be just as calamitous as the unchecked personality strengths of Napoleons and Hitlers.

The organization of psychological needs and styles of expression within personality is determined, to a significant extent, by the biogenetic constitutional givens of an individual. The interaction between personality variables, the situation, and subsequent social adaptations implies that biological factors are operating as well. Quantitative changes at the biogenetic level brought about by personality-environment interactions can have important social implications. For example, the conflict avoidance type, in seeking stability and meaning within low-conflict endeavours, tends to be highly attracted to family life. The opposite confrontative type, perhaps because of his affinity for long-range challenges and his capacity for independence, tends to rely less on family life and consequently have fewer children. Since the turn of the century, social structural factors in urban societies have been catalyzing the above variance in favour of the conflict avoidance type, which has been numerically increasing in the West. The Conflict Resolution Syndrome can therefore be viewed as a dynamic process operating at the biogenetic, personality, psychosocial, cultural, and historical levels.

The social and cultural implications of the Conflict Resolution Syndrome are disconcerting when seen in the light of the crucial problems and conflicts facing the world today. We are presently facing a population explosion, pollution and destruction of the ecology, urban congestion and its stresses, substance abuse and addiction, and the threat of a nuclear war. In order to avert crises with irreversible global repercussions, we require confrontative measures for these problems, not compromised solutions. The conflict avoidance type, with his flamboyant readiness to "solve" social problems and the short-range and inherent inadequacy of his approaches, may actually make these crises inevitable. For example, the anti-nuclear peace movement is not likely to have any significant success unless it transcends the theatrical exhibitionism that characterizes its present approach. A more organized political program must be adopted which is based on a comprehensive critical view of the social and political order. Individuals characterized by the Conflict Resolution Syndrome who often dominate peace movements may, by their superficiality and ineffectiveness, catalyze the ultimate violence: nuclear war.

The Romans had a saying: "if you want to maintain peace, prepare for war." In his book *The Biology of Peace and War* (1979), the eminent ethologist, Irenäus Eibl-Eibesfeldt, argued that "if you want to promote peace, study war." The research and theory presented in this book suggest an elaboration of the above recommendation: "if you want to promote peace, seek to understand not only war but also those incapable of war."

In the last two chapters I have attempted to depict the personal and social manifestations of the Conflict Resolution Syndrome. In the process of analysis, my value position regarding the social implications of the syndrome has revealed itself quite obviously. It is only through conscious awareness and explicit admission of one's values that, according to Max Weber, one can minimize their interference with scientific objectivity. My polemic perspective, dictated by my critical approach and by certain philosophical positions, should not have any bearing on the assessment of the validity of the constructs and variables advanced in this book, namely, the modes of conflict resolution and their pervasiveness within the personality, and the Conflict Resolution Syndrome. Future research can further refine these variables and, as was attempted in my research, investigate them in value-neutral areas of behaviour irrespective of their implications for society and the evaluation of these implications.

It has been said that the most important aspect of an inquiry is to ask the right questions. Techniques of investigation can always be found or improved upon but it is the path towards a different conceptualization that seems to be laden with anxiety, taboos, and idols. The social and human facts that are most difficult to see are those that lie near our noses. Therefore, in the asking of the right question intellectual courage is most important. I only hope that this book has managed to pose a relevant question.

APPENDIX

Table 1
Description of Subjects

Variable		Correctional Volunteers (N = 48)	Social Service Volunteers (N = 107)	Non-Volunteers (N = 170)
AGE	M	23.17	23.00	22.50
	SD	4.90	5.08	4.11
SEX	Male	22 (45.8%)	27 (25.2%)	74 (43.5%)
	Female	26 (54.2%)	80 (74.8%)	96 (56.5%)
MARITAL	Single	38 (79.2%)	82 (76.6%)	141 (82.2%)
STATUS	Married	9 (18.8%)	22 (20.6%)	22 (12%)
	Other	1 (2.1%)	3 (2.8%)	7 (4.1%)
EDUCATION	2	6 (12.5%)	18 (16.8%)	11 (6.5%)
(year at	3	16 (33.3%)	32 (29.9%)	69 (40.6%)
university)	4	26 (54.2%)	57 (53.3%)	90 (52.9%)
SPECIALIZATION (Major)	Social Sciences	37 (77.1%)	70 (65.4%)	102 (60%)
	Arts	3 (6.3%)	27 (25.3%)	34 (20%)
	Other	8 (16.7%)	10 (9.3%)	34 (20%)
ENROLLMENT	Full time	38 (79.2%)	91 (85.0%)	142 (83.5%)
	Part time	10 (20.8%)	16 (15.0%)	28 (16.5%)
EXPERIENCE AS VOLUNTEER	M	11.58	17.56	N.A.
(months)	SD	16.00	23.84	N.A.
VOLUNTEER WORK	M	4.83	5.38	N.A.
(hrs/wk)	SD	4.98	4.86	N.A.
AGE AT INITIAL VOLUNTEER	M	19.98	19.08	N.A.
WORK	SD	4.39	5.60	N.A.

Table 2
Means and Standard Deviations for Each Group on Each Measure

			Variables			
Group		Y_1	Y_2	Y_3	Y_4	Y_5
Non-Volunteers	M	51.96	12.64	1.54	22.84	2.91
(N = 170)	SD	8.94	5.81	1.33	5.36	0.55
Correctional Volunteers	M	47.12	10.14	1.33	21.77	2.32
(N = 48)	SD	10.55	4.78	1.22	6.55	0.48
Social Service	M	40.06	7.98	1.31	19.01	1.53
Volunteers (N = 107)	SD	9.35	4.71	1.27	5.77	0.51

Y_1 Intolerance of Ambiguity Scale
Y_2 Form Articulation Test
Y_3 Conceptual Systems Test
Y_4 Defining Issues Test
Y_5 Attitude to Political Violence Scale

Table 3
Summary of the Multivariate and Univariate Analysis of Variance Results for Correctional Volunteers and Non-Volunteers

Multivariate Hotelling's T = 0.031, df = (5,209), p-prob = 0.049					
Dependent Variable			Univariate ANOVA		
	Hyp. MS	df	Error MS	F	p-prob.
Intolerance of Ambiguity (Y_1)	304.79	(1,213)	86.89	4.20	0.041
Form Articulation (Y_2)	0.0	(1,213)	0.29	0.001	0.247
Conceptual Systems (Y_3)	60.37	(1,213)	15.72	3.84	0.049
Defining Issues (Y_4)	9.63	(1,213)	0.29	0.31	0.580
Political Violence (Y_5)	42.97	(1,213)	17.85	2.41	0.053

Table 4
Summary of the Multivariate and Univariate Analysis of Variance Results for Correctional Volunteers and Social Service Volunteers

Multivariate Hotelling's T = 0.029, df = (5,145), p-prob = 0.049					
Dependent Variable	Univariate ANOVA				
	Hyp. MS	df	Error MS	F	p-prob.
Intolerance of Ambiguity (Y_1)	282.52	(1,149)	108.39	2.61	0.051
Form Articulation (Y_2)	75.33	(1,149)	29.54	2.55	0.047
Conceptual Systems (Y_3)	0.18	(1,149)	0.25	0.72	0.398
Defining Issues (Y_4)	3.24	(1,149)	1.76	1.84	0.177
Political Violence (Y_5)	98.97	(1,149)	26.32	3.76	0.021

Table 5
Summary of the Multivariate and Univariate Analysis of Variance Results for Social Service Volunteers and Non-Volunteers

Multivariate Hotelling's T = 0.056, df = (5,264), p-prob = 0.013					
Dependent Variable	Univariate ANOVA				
	Hyp. MS	df	Error MS	F	p-prob.
Intolerance of Ambiguity (Y_1)	537.93	(1,268)	90.30	5.96	0.015
Form Articulation (Y_2)	90.58	(1,268)	33.32	2.72	0.100
Conceptual Systems (Y_3)	1.33	(1,268)	0.29	4.58	0.048
Defining Issues (Y_4)	102.93	(1,268)	16.82	6.12	0.021
Political Violence (Y_5)	114.42	(1,268)	30.47	3.75	0.051

BIBLIOGRAPHY

Abdennur, A. Violence as a function of abstract and cognitive processes. *Crime and justice*, 1979, *7*(2), 100-105.

Adorno, T.W., Frenkel-Brunswik, Else, Levinson, D.J., & Sanford, R.N. *The authoritarian personality*. New York: Harper, 1950.

Adsett, N.L. *Locus of control, self-concept and attitudes of parents of anonymous volunteers*. Doctoral dissertation. University of Toronto, 1976.

Algar, M.J., Hug, Z.T., & Lambert, L.R. *Assessment of the probation volunteer program in Metropolitan Toronto*. Toronto: Ministry of Correctional Services, 1975.

Allen, N.J., & Rushton, J.P. Personality characteristics of community mental health volunteers: A review. *Journal of voluntary action research*, 1983, *12* (1), 36-49.

Allport, G.W. *Pattern and growth in personality*. New York: Holt, Rinehart and Winston, 1961.

Allport, G.W. *Personality*. New York: Holt, Rinehart and Winston, 1937.

Almanzor, A.C. *Volunteer and staff participation in a voluntary social welfare association in the United States: A study of the National Y.W.C.A.* Doctoral dissertation, Columbia University, 1961.

American Psychiatric Association. *Diagnostic and statistical manual of mental disorders* (3rd ed.). Washington, D.C.: American Psychiatric Association, 1979.

Anderson, J.C., & Moore, L.F. Characteristics of Canadian volunteers in direct service. *Journal of voluntary action research*, 1974, *3*, 51-60.

Andrews, D., & Kiessling, J. Program structure and effective correctional practices: A summary of CAVIC research. In R.R. Ross & P. Gendreau, *Effective correctional treatment*. Toronto: Butterworths, 1980.

Andrews, D.A., Wormith, J.S., Kennedy, D.J., & Daigle-Zinn, W.J. The attitudinal effects of structured discussions and recreational association between young criminal offenders and undergraduate volunteers. *Journal of community psychology*, 1977, *5*, 63-71.

Arkell, N. Are student-helpers helped? *Psychology in the schools*, 1975, *12*, 113-115.

Barr, H. Motivation of volunteers in prison after-care. In H. Barr, *Volunteers in prison after-care*. London: Allen & Unwin, 1971.

Becker, H. *Outsiders: Studies in the sociology of deviance*. New York: Free Press, 1963.

Beckman, L. Locus of control and attitudes toward mental illness among mental health volunteers. *Journal of consulting and clinical psychology*, 1972, *38* (1), 84-89.

Bell, E., & Blakeney, R. Personality correlates of conflict resolution modes. *Human relations*, 1977, *30*, 849-857.

Bem, D.J., & Allen, A. On predicting some of the people some of the time: The search for cross-situational consistencies in behavior. *Psychological Review*, 1974, *81*, 506-520.

Block, J. Some reasons for the apparent inconsistency of personality. *Psychological Bulletin*, 1968, *70*, 210-212.

Bowers, K.S. Situationism in psychology: An analysis and a critique. *Psychological review*, 1973, *80*, 307-336.

Boyd, R.C. *The helper-therapy principle: A study of the effects of helping behavior on college student volunteers*. Doctoral dissertation, Purdue University, 1977.

Bronfenbrenner, U. Personality and participation: The case of vanishing variables. *Journal of social issues*, 1960, *16*, 54-63.

Budner, S. Intolerance of ambiguity as a personality variable. *Journal of personality*, 1962, *30*, 29-50.

Bullit, W., & Freud, S. *Thomas Woodrow Wilson: A psychological study*. (Manus, 1920), New York: Avon, 1968.

Case, J.D., & Henderson, J.F. Correctional volunteers in Bucks County. *American journal of correction*, 1973, January-February, 44-46.

Caldwell, M.M., Katz, M., & Levine, D. Characteristics of volunteers in a state mental hospital. *Volunteer administration*, 1972, *6* (1), 4-10.

Cattell, R.B. *Personality: A systematic, theoretical and factual study*. New York: McGraw-Hill, 1950.

Cattell, R.B. *The scientific analysis of personality*. Baltimore: Penguin Books, 1965.

Chartoff, S.I. *A comparison of interests, values, personality characteristics, and past experience with life crises of hotline volunteers, non-volunteers, and selected professional groups*. Doctoral dissertation, State University of New York, 1976.

Chinsky, J. *Non-professionals in a mental hospital*. Doctoral dissertation, University of Rochester, 1969.

Cleckley, H. *The mask of sanity*. Saint Louis: Mosby, 1976.

Cloward, R. Studies in tutoring. *Journal of experimental education*, 1967, *36*, 14-25.

Coleman, J.C., Butcher, J.N., & Carson, R.C. *Abnormal Psychology*. 6th ed. Glenview, Illinois: Foresman, 1980.

Consultation '81. Published by the National voluntary organizations, Ottawa, 1981.

Correctional Services of Canada. *Directory of volunteer programs in Canada.* Ottawa, 1986.

Coser, Lewis A. Conflict: Social aspects. *International encyclopedia of the social sciences.* D. Sills (Ed.). New York: Macmillan Company and the Free Press, Vol. 3, 1968.

Coser, Lewis A. *The functions of social conflict.* New York: Free Press, 1956.

Cull, J., & Hardy, R. (Eds.). *Volunteerism: An emerging profession.* Springfield, Ill.: C.C. Thomas, 1974.

Dahrendorf, R. *Class on class conflict in industrial society.* Stanford, California: Stanford University Press, 1959.

Davison, M.L., & Robbins, S. The reliability and validity of objective indices of moral development. *Applied psychological measurement,* 1978, *2* (3), 391-403.

Dawson, R.W.K. Personality and peer counsellors: An Australian study. *Personnel and guidance journal,* 1973, *52,* 46-49.

Deutsch, M. *The resolution of conflict: Constructive and destructive processes.* New Haven: Yale University Press, 1970.

Donahue, M.M. *Personality differences between volunteers and professionals.* Doctoral dissertation, St. John's University, 1969.

Doris, J. Social science and advocacy. *American behavioural scientist,* 1982, *26* (2), 199-233.

Dunn, S., & Langley, M. A radical critique of volunteerism in corrections. *Crime and justice,* 4 (1), 1976.

Durning, H.H. *Performance and perception in a volunteer program.* Doctoral dissertation, University of Colorado, 1974.

Eibl-Eibesfeldt, I. *The biology of peace and war.* Trans. E. Mosbacher. London: Thames and Hudson, 1979.

Endler, N.S. The person versus the situation: A response to Alker. *Journal of Personality,* 1973, *41,* 287-303.

Endler, N.S., & Magnusson, D. (Eds.) *Interactional psychology and personality.* New York: J. Wiley & Sons, 1976.

Endler, N., & Magnusson, D. (Eds.) *Personality at the crossroads: Current issues in interactional psychology.* Toronto: J. Wiley, 1977.

Engs, R.L.C. *The personality traits and health knowledge of crisis intervention volunteers in the state of Tennessee.* Doctoral dissertation, University of Tennessee, 1973.

Eriksson-Joslyn, Kerstin. A nation of volunteers: Participatory democracy or administrative manipulation? *Berkeley journal of sociology,* 1973-74, *18,* 159-181.

Eysenck, H.J. *The scientific study of personality.* London: Routledge and Kegan Paul, 1952.

Eysenck, H.J. *The psychology of politics*. London: Routledge and Kegan Paul, 1954.

Feinberg, L.B., & Sundblad, L. Need for approval and college student volunteers in community rehabilitation centers. *Rehabilitation counselling bulletin*, 1971, *14*, 245-251.

Feinstein, B., & Cavanaugh, C. *The new volunteerism*. Cambridge, Mass.: Schenkman Publishing, 1976.

Felknor, C., & Harvey, O.J. Parent-child relations as an antecedent to conceptual functioning. In O.J. Harvey (Ed.), *Early experiences and the processes of socialization*. New York: Academic Press, 1970.

Fisher, E.H. Who volunteers for companionship with mental patients? *Journal of personality*, 1971, *39*, 552-563.

Fleming, J. Pupil tutors and tutees learn together. *Today's education*, 1969, *58*, 22-24.

Frager, S., & Stern, C. Learning by teaching. *Reading teacher*, 1970, *23*, 403-405.

Frankl, Viktor. *Man's search for meaning*. Boston: Beacon Press, 1968.

Frankl, Viktor. *The unheard cry for meaning*. New York: Washington Square Press, 1978.

Frenkel-Brunswik, E. Intolerance of ambiguity as an emotional and perceptual personality variable. *Journal of personality*, 1949, *18*, 262-270.

Frenkel-Brunswik, E. Intolerance of ambiguity as an emotional and perceptual personality variable. In Bruner, J. & Krech, D. (Eds.), *Perception in personality*. New York: Greenwood Press, 1950.

Frenkel-Brunswik, E. Personality theory and perception. In Blake, R., & Ramsey, G. (Eds.), *Perception: an approach to personality*. New York: Ronald Press, 1951.

Frenkel-Brunswik, E. Further Explorations by a contributor to the authoritarian personality. In *The authoritarian personality: Scope and method*. R. Christie and M. Johoda, (Eds.), Glenco: Freepress, 1954, pp. 226-75.

Freud, S. *The future of an illusion* (1927). New York: Norton, 1975.

Freud, S. *Civilization and its discontents* (1928). New York: W. Norton, 1961.

Freud, S. *Letters*. E.L. Freud (Ed.). Translated by T. Stern. New York: Basic Books, 1961.

Friedman, M., & Rosenman, R.H. *Type A behavior and your heart*. New York: Knopf, 1974.

Fromm, Erich. *Escape from freedom*. New York: Rinehart, 1941.

Fromm, Erich. *The sane society*. New York: Holt, Rinehart & Winston, 1955.

Fromm, Erich. *Beyond the chains of illusion: My encounter with Marx and Freud.* New York: Simon & Shuster, 1962.

Gandy, J.M. Volunteers in four provincial adult correctional institutions. *Canadian journal of criminology and corrections,* 1977, *19,* 67-79.

Gartner, A., Kohler, M., & Riessman, F. *Children teach children.* New York: Harper & Row, 1971.

Goldstein, K. *Human nature in the light of psychopathology.* Cambridge, Mass.: Harvard University Press, 1940.

Guyatt, D.E. *The volunteer centre.* Toronto: Ministry of Community and Social Services, 1974.

Haan, Norma. Changes in young adults after peace corps experiences. *Journal of youth and adolescence,* 1974, *3* (3), 177-194.

Habenicht, D.L. *Descriptive study of the personality, attitudes, and overseas experience of Seventh-Day Adventist College students who served as short-term volunteer missionaries.* Doctoral dissertation, Andrews University, 1977.

Handler, J.S. Commitment to ideals and volunteer service. *American journal of psychotherapy,* 1968, *22* (4), 637-644.

Harris, L. Volunteers look at corrections. College Park, Maryland: American Correctional Association, 1969.

Harvey, O.J. Authoritarianism and conceptual functioning in varied conditions. *Journal of personality,* 1963, *31,* 462-470.

Harvey, O.J. Some cognitive determinants of influenceability. *Sociometry,* 1964, *27,* 208-221.

Harvey, O.J. Cognitive aspects of affective arousal. In S.S. Tomkins and C.E. Izard (Eds.), *Affect, cognition and personality.* New York: Springer, 1965.

Harvey, O.J. System structure, flexibility and creativity. Chapter 4 in O.J. Harvey (Ed.), *Experience, structure and adaptability.* New York: Springer, 1966.

Harvey, O.J. Conceptual systems and attitude change. In M. Sherif & C.W. Sherif (Eds.), *Attitude, ego-involvement and change.* New York: Wiley, 1967.

Harvey, O.J., & Ware, R. Personality differences in dissonance resolution. *Journal of personality and social psychology,* 1967, *7,* 227-230.

Hassinger, J., & Via, M. How much does a tutor learn through teaching reading. *Journal of secondary education,* 1969, *44,* 42-44.

Hawrylyshyn, O. The economic nature and value of volunteer activity in Canada. *Social indicators research,* 1978, *5* (1), 1-71.

Heckman, F. An investigation on the motivation of development aids. *Kölner zeitschrift für soziologie und sozialpsychologie,* 1974, *26* (1), 54-69.

Hersch, P.D., Kulik, J.A., & Scheibe, K.E. Personal characteristics of college volunteers in mental hospitals. *Journal of consulting and clinical psychology*, 1969, *33*, 30-35.

Hillman, K.G. *Volunteers in direct service: A study of their backgrounds and experiences*. Chicago, Volunteer Service Corps, 1967.

Hobfoll, S.E. Personal characteristics of the college volunteer. *American journal of community psychology*, 1980, *8* (4), 503-506.

Hoffmeister, J.K. *Conceptual systems test*. Boulder, Colorado: Test Analysis & Development Corporation, 1976.

Hofstadter, Richard. *Anti-intellectualism in American life*. New York: Alfred Knopf, 1966.

Holzberg, J.D., & Gerwitz, H.A. A method of altering attitudes towards mental illness. *Psychiatric supplement quarterly*, 1963, *37*, 56-61.

Holzberg, J.D., Gerwitz, H., & Ebner, E. Changes in moral judgement and self-acceptance of college students as a function of companionship with hospitalized mental patients. *Journal of consulting psychology*, 1964, *28*, 299-303.

Homans, George. *Social behavior: its elementary forms*. New York: Harcourt, 1961.

Horn, J.C. *Personality characteristics of direct service volunteers*. Doctoral dissertation, U.S. International University, 1973.

Hougland, James. Voluntary organizations and attitudes toward the community. *Sociological inquiry*, 1982, *52* (1) Winter, 53-70.

Howarth, E. Personality characteristics of volunteers. *Psychological reports*, 1976, *38* (3), 853-854.

Jaensch, E.R. *Der gegentypus*. Leipzig: Barth, 1938.

Jones, R.E., & Melcher, B.H. Personality and the preference for modes of conflict resolution. *Human relations*, 1982, *35* (8), 649-658.

Jung, Carl. *Psychological types*. New York: Harcourt, Brace & World, 1933.

Kelly, H.J. *The effect of the helping experience upon the self-concept of the helper*. Doctoral dissertation, University of Pittsburgh, 1974.

Kegerreis, J.P. *Congruence between volunteers' and coordinators' vocational needs, personality factors, and activity*. Doctoral dissertation, Texas Technical University, 1977.

King, M., Walder, L.O., & Pavey, S. Personality change as a function of volunteer experience in a psychiatric hospital. *Journal of consulting and clinical psychology*, 1970, *35* (3), 428-435.

Kluge, C.A. *An investigation of personality variables, needs, and helping styles of non-professional volunteers in a telephone crisis intervention center*. Doctoral dissertation, Texas Technical University, 1974.

Knapp, J.I., & Holzberg, J.D. Characteristics of college students volunteering for service to mental patients. *Journal of consulting and clinical psychology*, 1964, *28*, 82-85.

Knowles, M.S. Motivation in volunteerism: Synopsis of a theory. *Journal of voluntary action research*, 1972, *1* (2), 27-29.

Kohlberg, L. Stage and sequence: The cognitive developmental approach to socialization. In D. Gostein (Ed.), *Handbook of socialization: Theory and research*. Chicago: Rand McNally, 1969.

Kohlberg, L. Foreword. In J. Rest, *Development in judging moral issues*. Minneapolis: University of Minnesota Press, 1979.

Koopman, E.J. *Identity formation processes in volunteer and non-volunteer university students*. Doctoral dissertation, University of Maryland, 1973.

Labaté, L., & Milan, M. (Eds.), *Handbook of social skills training and research*. New York: John Wiley, 1985.

Landrun, J., & Martin, M. When students teach others. *Educational Leadership*, 1970, *27*, 446-448.

Lasch, Christopher. *Culture of narcissism*. New York: Warner Books, 1979.

Lazarus, R.S., & Monat, A. *Personality* (3rd ed.). Englewood Cliffs, New Jersey: Prentice-Hall, 1979.

Link, Henry C. *The return to religion*. New York: Macmillan, 1936.

Lorenz, C. *On aggression*. New York: Harcourt, 1966.

Macaulay, J., & Berkowitz, L. *Altruism and helping behavior: Social psychological studies of some antecedents and consequences*. New York: Academic Press, 1970.

Marcuse, Herbert. *Eros and civilization; A philosophical inquiry into Freud*. London: Sphere Books, 1956.

Marcuse, Herbert. *One Dimensional man*. Boston: Beacon Press, 1964.

Marcuse, H., Moore, B., & Wolf, R. *A critique of pure tolerance*. Boston: Beacon Press, 1965.

McClelland, D.C. *Personality*. New York: Dryden Press, 1951.

McKian, P.J. *Shifts in self-concept and locus of control in college students as a function of volunteering with emotionally disturbed children*. Doctoral dissertation, University of Chicago, 1977.

Mehl, Dominique. The political culture of voluntary associations. *Sociologie du travail*, 1982, *24*, 24-42.

Miller, T.W. Internal-external locus of control and attitudes toward mental illness in non-professional mental health workers. *Personality and social psychology bulletin*, 1974a, *1* (1), 357-358.

Miller, R.S. The future of volunteer action. In J. Cull and R. Hardy (Eds.), *Volunteerism: An emerging profession*. Springfield, Ill.: C.C. Thomas, 1974b.

Mills, C.W. *The power elite*. New York: Galaxy Press, 1956.

Ministry of Correctional Services, Province of Ontario. *Annual report*, 1984. Toronto: Parliament Buildings, Queen's Park.

Ministry of the Solicitor General of Canada. *Basic facts about corrections.* Ottawa: Communications Branch, 1984.

Mischel, W. Continuity and change in personality. *American psychologist,* 1969, *24,* 1012-1018.

Mischel, W. *Personality and assessment.* New York: Wiley, 1968.

Murray, H.A. *Explorations in personality.* New York: Oxford University Press, 1938.

Nassi, A., & Abramowitz, S. From phrenology to psychosurgery and back again: biological studies of criminality. *American journal of orthopsychiatry,* 1976, *46* (4), 590-607.

Nietzsche, F. *Beyond good and evil* (1885). Trans. by H. Zimmern. New York: Russell, 1964.

Nietzsche, F. *On the genealogy of morals* (1887). Trans. by H. Samuel. New York: Russell, 1964.

O'Connor, P. Ethnocentrism, intolerance of ambiguity and abstract reasoning ability. *Journal of abnormal psychology,* 1952, *47,* 526-530.

Park, R.G., & Burgess, E. *Introduction to the science of society.* Chicago: University of Chicago Press, 1924.

Parsons, R., & Wicks, R. (Eds.) *Passive-aggressiveness.* New York: Brunner/Mazel, 1983.

Payne, R., Payne, B.P., & Reddy, R.D. Social background and role determinants of individual participation in organized voluntary action. In D.H. Smith, R.D. Reddy, & B.R. Baldwin (Eds.), *Voluntary action research.* Lexington, Mass.: Heath, 1972, 207-250.

Penner, L.A. *Social Psychology: A contemporary approach.* New York: Oxford University Press, 1978.

People in action: Report of the National Advisory Council on Voluntary Action to the Government of Canada, 1977.

Pervin, L.A. *Personality: theory, assessment and research.* New York: Wiley, 1975.

Phares, E.J. *Locus of control: A personality determinant of behavior.* Morristown, New Jersey: General Learning Press, 1973.

Pierucci, J., & Noel, R.C. Duration of participation of correctional volunteers as a function of personal and situational variables. *Journal of community psychology,* 1980, *8,* 245-250.

Pollock, Phillip. Organizations and alienation: The mediation hypothesis revisited. *The sociological quarterly,* 1982, *23* (2), 143-155.

Reddy, R.D., & Smith, D.H. Why do people participate in voluntary action? *Journal of extension,* 1973, *11* (4), 35-40.

Rest, J.R. *Revised manual for the defining issues test: An objective test of moral judgement development.* Minneapolis, Minnesota: Moral Research Projects, 1979a.

Rest, J.R. *Development in judging moral issues.* Minneapolis: University of Minnesota Press, 1979b.

Rest, J.R., Davison, M.L., & Robbins, S. Age trends in judging moral issues: A review of cross-sectional, longitudinal, and sequential studies of the defining issues test. *Child development,* 1978, *49* (2), 263-279.

Riessman, F. The helper therapy principle. *Social work,* 1965, *10,* 27-65.

Rokeach, M. *The open and closed mind.* New York: Basic Books, 1960.

Rosenthal, R., & Rosnow, R.L. *The volunteer subject.* New York: Wiley-Interscience Publication, 1975.

Ross, R.R., & McKay, H.B. A study of institutional treatment programs. *International journal of offender therapy and comparative criminology,* 1976, *20* (2), 167-173.

Rotter, J.B. Generalized expectancies for internal versus external control of reinforcement. *Psychological Monographs.* 1966, *80* (609).

Roupe, Diane. What it means to be a volunteer. *Rehabilitation records,* January-February, 1973, 9-12.

Sager, W.G. *A study of changes in attitudes, values, and self-concepts of senior high youth while working as full-time volunteers with institutionalized mentally retarded people.* Doctoral dissertation, University of South Dakota, 1974.

Saunders, D.H. Some preliminary interpretive material for the PRI. *Research memorandum 55-15.* Educational Testing Service, October, 1955.

Sayre, Cynthia. The impact of voluntary associations involvement on social-psychological attitudes. *American sociological association* (ASA), 1980, 3096.

Schachter, S. Deviation, rejection and communication. In D. Cartwright and A. Zander (Eds.), *Group Dynamics: Research and Theory.* New York: Harper & Row, 1968.

Schnidler-Rainman, E. The volunteer citizen of the seventies. In *Proceedings: new approaches to working with volunteers.* University of British Columbia, Centre for Continuing Education, November 1972.

Scioli, F.P., & Cook, T.J. How effective are volunteers? Public participation in the criminal justice system. *Crime and delinquency,* 1976, April, 192-200.

Selznick, Philip. *Tennessee valley authority and the grass roots: A study in the sociology of formal organizations* (first pub. 1953). New York: Harper, 1966.

Simmel, George. *Conflict: The web of group affiliations* (1908). Glencoe, Illinois: Free Press, 1955.

Simonton, O.C. *Getting well again.* Los Angeles: J.P. Tracher, 1978.

Skinner, B.F. Behaviorism at fifty. *Science*, 1963, *140*, 951-958.

Smith, B.M.M., & Nelson, L.D. Personality correlates of helping behavior. *Psychological reports*, 1975, *37*, 307-310.

Smith, D.H. *Types of volunteers and volunteerism*. Volunteer Administration, 1972, *6*, 3-10.

Smith, D.H. Research and communication needs in voluntary action. In J. Cull and R. Hardy (Eds.), *Volunteerism: An emerging profession*. Springfield, Ill.: C.C. Thomas, 1974.

Sorel, Georges. *Réflexion sur la violence* (first pub. 1907). Paris: M. Rivière, 1972.

Starr, J.M. *Cross-cultural encounter and personality change: Peace corps volunteers in the Philippines*. Doctoral dissertation, Brandeis University, 1970.

Statistics Canada. *Overview of volunteer work in Canada*. Labor Force Survey, No. 26, 1981.

Staub, E. *Positive social behaviour and morality*. Vol. 1 & 2. New York: Academic Press, 1978.

Steiner, T.F. *An investigation of motivational factors operative in prosocial volunteers*. Doctoral dissertation, United States International University, 1975.

Tapp, J.T., & Spanier, D. Personal characteristics of volunteer phone counsellors. *Journal of consulting and clinical psychology*, 1973, *41* (2), 245-250.

Turner, J.R. *Volunteer participation as a function of personal and situational variables*. Doctoral dissertation, University of Utah, 1972.

Wallston, B.S. *Community human resources development in the rehabilitation of the handicapped*. Nashville: Outlook, 1972.

Ware, R., & Harvey, O.J. A cognitive determinant of impression formation. *Journal of personality and social psychology*, 1967, *5*, 38-44.

Welsh, G.S. *Welsh figure preference test: research edition*. Palo Alto: Consulting Psychologists Press, Inc., 1959.

Whalen, Thelma. Wives of alcoholics. Reprinted from *Journal of Studies on Alcohol*, 1953, *14*, 632-641. Copyright in W. Rushing (Ed.), *Deviant Behavior and Social process*. Rand McNally College Publishing Co., 1975.

White, B.J., & Harvey, O.J. Effects of personality and own stand on judgement and production of statements about a central issue. *Journal of experimental and social psychology*, 1965, *1*, 334-347.

Witkin, H. *Psychological differentiation: Studies of development*. New York: Wiley, 1962.

Zimbardo, P. The human choice. In *Nebraska symposium on motivation*. Volume XVII. Lincoln, Nebraska: University of Nebraska Press, 1969.